Forget everything you've been taught.
Master your ego and your fears.
Release your natural creativity.
Lead through chaos from your purpose.

Unleadership

Towards a more Human Leadership in times of Artificial Intelligence.

Jesús Hijas

Prologue by Carmen Bustos

Edition: Jesús Hijas

To my Polar Star
and the guardians of its trail.

Index

Part III. Release your natural creativity.

Part IV. Lead through chaos from your purpose.

Outro. A space for reflection.

Hannah Mc

Prologue

The book you are holding in your hands talks about the real challenge that we have as a society at this time: human leadership.

Perhaps you feel overwhelmed by all the technological changes that we are facing, because of its speed and ability to transform absolutely everything. You will probably find yourself with the need to understand these changes and invest time to study them in detail and understand how they will affect you. It is reasonable. But let me share a reflection with you: behind technology there are people and the positive or negative impact of what is happening and is yet to come depends solely and exclusively on people and our ability to lead change.

Today, therefore, it is more urgent than ever to reflect on the figure of the leader, understanding by leader any person who has to make decisions about life, profession and business. That includes you as well, and me, because we all must be leaders of our own personal and professional adventures and, most importantly, because the leadership style as we knew it until now is practically obsolete.

This book presents you a journey that will help you transform that ancient vision of leadership into a truly transformative one. A journey that will release your creative potential to reach a more human, genuine and impactful leadership. A journey where you are going to be the protagonist and whose ending will depend entirely on your desire and your frankness.

My recommendation is that you take this opportunity to be honest with yourself, that you invest quality time to reflect and seek answers to the questions that, in a simple and natural way, this journey will be asking you.

Revealing points that, probably, at some stage have come to mind but that, due to lack of time or even courage, you have not finished solving.

Without a doubt, for me, the best thing about this experience has been the honesty with which Jesús has written this book. Reading these pages and seeing how everything he shares in them is an accurate reflection of the journey that he has lived previously, makes me feel super proud to have had the opportunity to meet, work together and keep learning from each other.

This book makes the word *authenticity*, so empty of meaning in the current context, recover its value and amplify itself. Because Jesús does not intend to give us a perfect and theoretical recipe, quite the opposite. In an absolutely generous way, he shares with us his learnings and every step he has taken during his own journey in an authentic and very practical way, so that you can take what you think can help you and put aside what doesn't convince you.

His story represents the journey that many professionals, like you, face today. A journey of change and search inside yourself, but also a journey where to make sense of what surrounds you and what you do. With a clear objective: that you are able to successfully lead any project that you consider in your life once you have recovered or discovered your purpose, that polar star that will make you make the best decisions, being faithful to your principles, with joy and confidence.

The world needs new references, leaders who, with true passion and values, embark on new paths with meaning, height and depth towards a fairer, more sustainable and more human world.

Jesús is certainly one of them and I have no doubt that you can be as well. Now, I just want you to enjoy it and dare to be brave like he was. I am sure it will be worth it.

Carmen Bustos

Founder and leader of Soulsight - *Innovation and Design Strategy* and of Wanderbeing - The first global school of human leadership.

COSTES - INVERSIONES - COST DE OPOR

NO   PASSION

IN EQUAL → out of passion.
↳ LabTech.

Intro.   Strategic reasons to not split break

discern   exceed your capacity or your role capacity

Why I have written this book and why you should read it... or not.

Mentor

I NEED PASSION   Nathan is Nathan   Hay alternativas

ARTICULAR   NO MORE NB

C L A R I T Y   7' 7'

NB no esté   Si tú haces sin pasión salen
GM esté

TRUSO PLAN NATHAN /FLIP

7'

Possibly, the term *leadership* is one of the most hackneyed, overused, deconstructed, idealized, repeated and not always well used in the modern business world. And, somehow, we all feel that we exercise good leadership. Let us admit it. When one sees the typical post on Linkedin that says "Boss vs Leader" and lists how each one acts, regarding aspects such as recognition, crisis management, communication style, motivation or attitude, one would think, "Well, I am a good leader. And my boss is a… boss."

But what is being a good leader? Is it something that applies only to those we call bosses, who have people under their charge? Is it a thing for entrepreneurs? Is it something that is limited exclusively to the professional field? Can you be a good leader without being a good father or mother, partner or person? Can you be a good leader by forgetting your own passions? Can you be a good leader if you feel, on a daily basis, that you are not doing what you could or want to do in your life?

Until recently, I considered myself a good leader. Then, I started to ask myself these and many other questions and to seek sincere answers. And I began a journey that proved me wrong concerning the many basic aspects of life that shape the way we lead, either others or ourselves. That journey changed my life.

Thanks to that journey, today I know that in order to lead other people with the authenticity demanded by the economy of trust and the era of Artificial Intelligence, we must lead them by the example of who we are: to lead from the inside out, without artificial masks. That there are not two people -the professional *self* and the personal *self*- and that living in congruence with who you are is something that goes beyond all work or short-term need. That passions move us from within with more energy than external factors such as titles, positions or money can offer us. To lead the present of constant revolution and evolution that we have to live, we must remain curious, attentive, humble, sensitive, and vulnerable, with an attitude of constant listening and help, active, honest, and open to failure, in a position to learn continuously.

This attitude makes me wake up every day with the innocence of a child who is going to learn everything the world wants to teach him and with the will of an adult who is going to connect all these learnings to lead his own path. With humility but with determination. With endless curiosity and with a backpack loaded with experiences. Recognizing and boosting the emotions that define us as human beings and with emotional intelligence. In constant search and congruence.

Along this path I found out, among other things, that leadership, far from being a matter for bosses or entrepreneurs, is an essential skill for every human being, as the human mind needs to understand reality in order to survive and transform it to be happy.

All human beings need to take action, be leaders to understand and transform the reality that surrounds us. Your mind, which wants to survive and be happy, needs to lead.

In this way, the word *leadership* went long ago in my head from being a monotonous term and without credibility, to being a universal human need with the capability to move restless minds towards collective purposes. A term worth recovering. That is why *Unleadership* is born.

This is my story. And I am so keen on spreading the word, that I have the same enthusiasm as a child painting on a blank sheet, who does it for the love of art, without minding if someone is going to spend some time to see his drawing, value it, or let alone pay for it.

However, it seems fair to me to dedicate at least half of this *Intro* so that you, who are looking at my drawing, have some more information about whether you want to continue devoting your time to seeing it or if you would rather invest it on something else. Among other things, because nowadays technology allows us to have access to hundreds of thousands of responses in a matter of milliseconds. And, among other things, because your time is the most valuable thing you possess, and your choice of how to use it, the only thing you actually have.

Therefore, I am going to dig a little bit deeper into this initial introspective that I want to invite you in before starting this journey. And I am going to do so by sharing with you, in the first person, that universal tool that played an essential part in my transformation and that, in my experience, a few use and very few use it well: the question.

Would you take the job you are passionate about for half the salary?

Moreover, would you take the job you are passionate about without receiving any salary at all?

Moreover, would you work without salaray for turning what you are passionate about into a job in the future?

I invite you to think of these questions and seek an honest answer (the only one you can give yourself) while I give you some keys as to why I ask you these in the *Intro* of this book.

This is not a book about entrepreneurship. Although if you have answered "yes" to the three previous questions, you probably have a lot of what is called Entrepreneurial Attitude, and that has to do with Leadership. And, although the term Entrepreneurship also suffers a lot from the evil of public tampering, *a.k.a. trending topic*, I believe that the future of work will be less in the hands of conformist companies and more in the hands of brave entrepreneurs, who choose to live off their passions, own their time, work with joy for collective, sustainable and meaningful causes, and maintain its authenticity and independence. And I believe it because that awareness and creativity will be the skills with which these entrepreneurs will lead that future of work in the era of Artificial Intelligence. So yes, we will talk about entrepreneurship, intrapreneurship and Entrepreneurial Attitude.

This is not a book about money. Although we will speak of money. After all, we live in a society where we need money to live. The previous three questions are very well selected, among many others that this journey will ask you, because they address the two key blocks that, in my opinion, prevent people from leading their own path in life: the ego and fear. And usually, after both blocks, there is the money.

This is not a book on technology. Although technological progress is the engine that is bringing about the changes that we live as a society and as a species, and whose acceleration has exceeded the threshold of what is bearable by the models currently established in all aspects of society. Therefore, we will talk about technology.

This is not a book on *mindfulness*. Although we live in a time when the demand for immediacy, *multitasking* and permanent hyper-connectivity have taken over our day-to-day lives, they make us go like automatons and have blurred our sense of consciousness, the way we lead our professional and personal lives and, consequentially, our well-being. In this context, the application of the essential principles of *mindfulness* - serene, lucid and equanimous attention (without judgment) - become the basis of conscious leadership that we must recover, today more than ever. We will therefore speak of *mindfulness* and its fundamental principles will help us throughout the book.

This is not a book on leadership. Not exclusively. Not about the leadership that we have understood so far. Although we will lean on the interpretation that many have made of this term, especially in the traditional executive world, as a mere excuse to establish their own control mechanisms. A style that has simply expired, opening the door for the term Leadership to permeate naturally, without interested barriers, into other disciplines such as self-knowledge, creativity, emotion, critical independence, collective sustanability or meaningful communication. Inherently human disciplines where the term Leadership acquires a horizontal and universal dimension, becoming an essential skill for people in the era of Artificial Intelligence.

Unleadership is a journey.

A one-way journey to the bottom of your consciousness, in which you will have to overcome many fears and egos that you have imposed on yourself and many mantras that the society in which you live has imposed on you. A journey in which you will see everything that does not work in the current system but that you have assumed almost without realizing it and that will change you forever.

And a journey back to your day-to-day reality, which neither has changed nor wants to change, and in which you will have to take action so that the findings of your consciousness have meaning and you can transform your reality and lead it.

Unleadership is a first-person journey, because there is no transformation possible without first activating intrapersonal intelligence, that of self-knowledge and self-awareness, which is within each one of us; and, from that awareness of the *self*, employ interpersonal intelligence to lead the *ourselves*, inspiring and collaborating with other people in a natural way for a collective purpose and with the same values to transform reality for the better for everyone.

Unleadership is a journey that I did in the first person, with no other guidance than a strong will to change, my intuition and the significant get-together with certain people whose testimonies are collected here. It transformed me forever and I felt that I had to share it to help others to travel their own journey.

Unleadership is the practical approach with which I propose to return the term *leadership* to its rightful place in the 21st century, the era in which people play a card that the world, the place where we live, to be a more human place.

Part I.

Forget everything you 've been taught.

Within the everyday, something happens and works as a call to action. Duty, obligations, insecurity, weakness, fear, influence so that the hero rejects the call and prefers to remain as he is. But finally, necessarily, he must embark on the adventure, delving into an unknown and dangerous terrain in which there are no known rules or limitations.

Chapter 1

VUCA.

You may know the term VUCA. It makes me laugh because it is one of those acronyms by which a consultant will have enriched himself, but it does nothing more than expressing an obvious reality. VUCA is an acronym that in English refers to:

V	*Volatile*
U	*Uncertain*
C	*Complex*
A	*Ambiguous*

This is the world we live in today:

Volatile, since what today is tomorrow may not be (for example, an incumbent company in the *Retail* sector a few years ago, that did not see Amazon coming).

Uncertain, since there are more and more factors that make something not happen 100% or 0% (for example, the fact that an engineer, a doctor or even an official today in Spain has a guaranteed job for life).

Complex, because understanding the reality of any business today implies understanding new environments, actors and channels that apparently did not influence before (for example, the local business whose sales depended entirely on physical visits to stores and that now invoice more than half of its sales thanks to product tagging on Instagram).

Ambiguous, because societies no longer see things white or black, blue or red, in masculine or feminine, but there is an intermediate gray scale that breaks through (for example, the fact that 55% of young people called Generation Z declare that they do not identify as *exclusively heterosexuals*).

Many aspects of the world we know are changing today. Society, work, business, human relations, the relationship with the planet, human consciousness itself. It is like if all these aspects have become completely liquid and would be changing today faster than ever.

Why this greater speed? Our society, work, business, relationships... all are aspects that have always been in constant evolution. Why is it different now? What has changed so that the world today has this feeling of constant revolution? What has changed so that people today have that need for continuous adaptation so we are not left out?

Change is the new normal, says the slogan that some assign to our time. The answer to these questions is, most certainly, technology.

Chapter 2

Technology changes your life every day.

Frequently, to understand what is happening in the present, it is helpful to look back and understand what has happened in the past. We wonder why our era is the era of constant change.

Think about the following:

In the 70s, no one had a personal computer at home. Nowadays, the number of households around the world with a personal computer represents roughly 50% of the total.

In the 80s, very few had a mobile phone (and these few "mobiles" actually weighed almost 1 kg and were each 33 cm long). Nowadays, more than 66% of the world population has a mobile phone. In Spain, in fact, there are more mobiles than there are people.

Until the *World Wide Web* (www) was launched on August 6, 1991, the Internet was something unknown to the world (even after that date it was, since no one then came on stage to tell us how the Internet was going to turn our lives upside down). Today 3.5 billion people around the world (that is 45% of the world population) have access to the Internet, find answers and information instantly, communicate with people no matter what their location is, shop without leaving home.

Apple released its first iPhone model in 2007. Until then, having a touchscreen on a phone that did smart things was a futuristic movies thing. Today the penetration of the *smartphone* globally is 33%.

In the following graphic, called *Waves of Innovation* and belonging to the study *The Natural Edge Project* by Bain Consulting, we see the 6 long waves of innovation that, in the last 250 years, have changed the world and what those innovations have been.

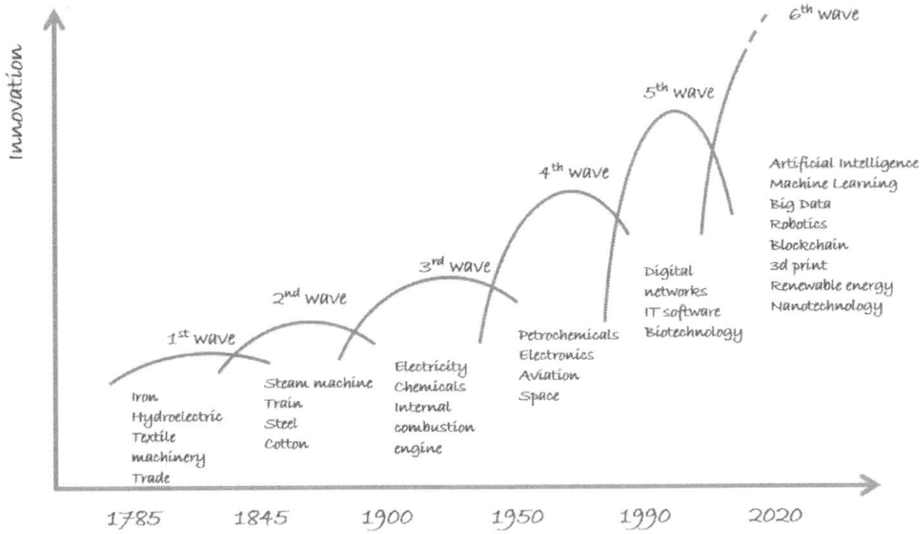

We call *innovation* to any change that introduces new developments and that modifies existing elements or processes in order to improve or renew them. In this context, we allude to the great innovations that had a high impact on people's lives, since they changed the way they lived.

The study tells us how each of these so-called Innovation Waves destroyed jobs, transforming them or creating new ones, and how in each and every one of these periods of technological disruption, this process created a feeling of panic in societies due to the radical changes to which people were exposed.

Does it ring a bell? We are talking about the introduction of commerce, the steam engine, electricity, electronics or the internet, but it seems that this pattern has not changed. Panic over change. This is the case today.

As we said before, what has changed? Why is it different now?

The Internet has changed the rules of the game. The digital revolution, besides a disruption in itself, is a platform for other revolutions to occur. Before the Internet, only a few people with access to the necessary resources could create the next revolution. Textile machinery, steam engine, electricity. And this happened every 60, 50, 40 years. After the arrival of the Internet, the rules of the game change because the Internet allows instant access to any connected person in the world or any information that is on the network. Since the Phoenicians introduced trade, the only innovation that had occurred in the distribution of goods (what we now call products and services) had to do with transportation, that is to say, with reducing the physical delivery time of those goods. From ships to road transport by horses and carriages, to trains, to motor vehicles. But the Internet takes distribution to another dimension: instantaneity. Time 0. Products and services are not distributed physically but digitally, so they do not depend on transport to be delivered. In fact, we changed their name: digital products and services.

And not only does the distribution change, but also the production. Anyone with a computer connected to the Internet and notions of programming can produce, create digital products. Furthermore, it can produce digital services so that other people connected to the Internet, but without programming notions, can participate in this new digital productive economy (this is the case of any *Marketplace* or platform such as Amazon, Wallapop, Fiverr or Airbnb, where anyone who has a good, product or service can offer it on these platforms in order to find a buyer, customer or tenant).

There is something very interesting about *The Natural Edge Project*'s waves of innovation chart. And it is that the time that an era lasts, is progressively shortened. For example, the Iron Age lasts approximately 60 years until steel arrives. The era of the steam engine lasts for about 55 years until it is replaced by the combustion engine, which in turn lasts for about 50 years until the next revolution arrives. The waves of innovation are shortened. From 60 years to 50 to 40 to 30. This means that before, a person could live his entire working life within the same era, working with the same technology (whatever depending on the sector). At most, he had to go through a technological revolution and the adaptation that this brings forth. And, although we know that many did not achieve that adaptation, we are talking about that: a single adaptation.

However, today technological revolutions arrive in a much shorter time. Think that:

Until 2007, *smartphones* did not exist.

Until 2008, *app stores* did not exist.

Until 2009, WhatsApp did not exist.

Until 2010, Instagram did not exist.

All of them, technologies massively adopted today. In the digital age (the age of the Internet), services and new technologies are launched every year that thanks to instant distribution, can rapidly become massive and grow exponentially in a few years, completely changing people's habits and, therefore, the competitive horizon for any company in basically any sector.

In the era we live in, the chances of another great technological revolution landing and completely changing the rules of the game are huge. Augmented Reality, Virtual Reality, Blockchain, 3D Printing, Nanotechnology, Artifical Intelligence. All are recent technologies with a high potential for disruption.

Among all these technological revolutions, I am especially interested in Artificial Intelligence, defined as "the intelligence of machines, the behavior of computer systems programmed to perceive the environment and execute actions to maximize their chances of success in some objective or task, and that they imitate human cognitive functions such as learning".

We are indeed talking about machines that learn. Or, as they are technically named, *Machine Learning* systems. In recent years, we have already been in contact with these systems: the way in which Google adapts and improves the results of its searches based on the parameters of user behavior (such as other searches, clicks on links that are of his interest, and many other parameters such as his location and movement pattern) or how Facebook, Linkedin or Twitter prioritize the information presented to the user, whether it comes from their organic network or from a network of advertisers, according to his behavior within those networks (interests, contacts, biography...). But also, progressively, the way in which our bank or our connectivity company recommends us or promotes products, services or rates, or adapts the attention it offers us as customers.

Up until now, we had used machines to solve algorithmic problems, that is to say, those problems whose solution is known and can be achieved by applying a series of steps or tasks (this sequence of tasks is what is called an algorithm; for example, the mechanism of a washing machine is an algorithm since, through a sequence of steps, it provides a solution to a known problem -clean the dirty clothes-). Artificial Intelligence now also approaches the resolution of heuristic problems, that is to say, those problems for which the solution is not known and, therefore, could not exist, there might be a single solution or there might be multiple solutions. Artificial Intelligence establishes trees of possibilities by exploring, acquiring new knowledge and adding it to the existing set of knowledge to delimit the problem on which to re-explore and learn, thus maximizing its chances of success in formulating possible solutions. In other words, Artificial Intelligence has the ability to reprogram itself constantly thanks to what it learns.

If we look at the definition of "human being", we find that the human being is a species "that possesses mental capacities that allow it to invent, learn and use complex linguistic and logical structures, mathematics, writing, music, science and technology; humans are social animals, capable of conceiving, transmitting and learning totally abstract concepts."

Both definitions (Artificial Intelligence and Human Being) have learning as a common central element. This is the great advance and at the same time the great dilemma posed by Artificial Intelligence: it is a technology to imitate the most essentially human behaviors, in particular learning. Where this will take us is currently one of the most interesting discussion topics.

Technology changes our life every day. It has been doing it for centuries. But, while until now the great technological revolutions occurred every 50, 40 or 30 years, today the Internet allows a new revolution to emerge basically at any time. And, while until now technology has been automating processes and mechanical tasks that people executed in specific specialization environments, today Artificial Intelligence is born to replicate what defines us more deeply and essentially as human beings.

This is the reason why, in the era of constant technological revolution and, particularly, Artificial Intelligence, people having their brains *programmed* to relearn continuously, is not an option but an obligation for survival. This is the great difference of our present. And it is one of the biggest challenges that we have as a species.

Chapter 3

We have been educated for the world of yesterday.

It is said of those born in the 90s and in the years thereafter (the so-called Generation Z) that they only understand life in digital, an environment in which everything is immediate and everything changes in a second, with a *tweet*. Something that makes sense if we think that they were born in a context of innovation and constant change, which has also been mixed with one of the biggest economic and social crises across the world since 1929.

It is said of the Generation Z that they have the ability, the habit and, most importantly, the desire to build from scratch repeatedly; that they are non-conformists by nature, because they have grown up in an environment that is Volatile, Uncertain, Complex and Ambiguous, and their mind has needed it to survive. In other words, *they are programmed* to relearn. Constantly.

Those born in the 60s, 70s, even 80s (that is to say, the vast majority of the current *workforce*) have been educated in the search for stability, security, things that last *a lifetime*. Degree. Job. Marriage. Home. It is as if before there was a script of life written for everyone and they had taught us that the secret of happiness was solving its chapters one by one. *To be set for life.*

It is hardly surprising, since the educational model that we have had in the schools of the late twentieth century, is more similar to a military training or the preparation of workers for a factory, than to the search and empowerment of talents and personal passions of each individual. The instructional model of the Prussian army looked for docile, replicable and replaceable soldiers, capable of executing orders without thinking, at a speed theoretically insurmountable by other armies (an aspect that Napoleon took advantage of in battle, causing situations of pressure or chaos in which the Prussian army had no capacity for independent initiative). In this system, soldiers acquire specific skills and progress through predefined general instructional blocks until completing it. Those who have completed the training progress. Those who do not succeed are excluded. When a soldier is no longer eligible for battle due to age, disability, or death, he is easily replaced by another soldier.

The funny thing is that the instructional model of the Prussian army had been quickly exported to other countries and ended up forming the basis of what, subsequently and until practically today, would be known as the educational system.

The industrial labor system does not differ much from this. Workers who have been educated in a definite specialization and who are imposed general rules to maximize productivity: hours, position, general guidelines for behavior... Replicable and replaceable workers. Let us not look for signs of empowerment of motivation and individual talent in this model.

Perhaps, the fact that the large technological waves covered then, as we have seen, at least the years of a generation, was enough to think that a person could live on his specific training throughout life by being educated in a fixed context and specializing in a certain subject. And maybe it worked for a while.

But this is simply no longer the case. The context is radically different and we have been left in no man's land, educated for a world that has become extinct and without the necessary skills to face the one that lies ahead. How can we live with security and stability as models of happiness if the only constant in the current context is change?

We need a paradigm shift. A new model in which human intelligence is structured to understand change and oriented to lead it continuously.

Let us not think that the responsibility for transformation falls exclusively on education. This is obvious to me and, although I think that there is much to be done, I have verified with pleasure how educational models and the *mindset* are changing in children's centers: empowerment of multiple intelligences, work through collaborative projects, acceptance of diversity, promotion of critical and creative independent thinking, etc. Which is a very important first step. But let us remember that this generation that is in school today is already, somehow, *reprogrammed.*

The generation that needs *to be reprogrammed* is currently working; it has its responsibilities and its positions, its ties and its aspirations that, in many cases, will have to do with the search for a stability that no longer exists.

Companies have a great responsibility in this transformation, in this paradigm shift. Companies are seeing the context change brutally and living its consequences. The solution is not only to incorporate new talent, with a mind more adapted to change and less ties. But to create a corporate culture in which change is encouraged and becomes something recognized and natural.

I find this point interesting. The responsibility of companies - more specifically, their leaders - in transforming people so that they are capable of relearning, leading, living and being happy in an environment of constant change. Therefore, I am going to delve a little more into it.

Chapter 4

The leader of the 20th century.

In this context of constant change and uncertainty, it might seem that we live in absolute chaos in the city of Gotham. Apparently, it is not the case. The sun rises every morning, the buildings in the cities are still standing, and the water comes out clean from the tap.

However, there is something that does not fit in. Something that we cannot see. A feeling within us, many of us, that tells us that something does not work.

We live in the age of lack of time. This call for wanting to have everything here and now has transformed human relationships. It is possible that technology is in the focus of this transformation, since the internet and the digital world have brought that possibility, which is now a necessity, of immediacy to people. However, I think that people are the ones who have not been able to take it on the positive side. It is not acceptable for Google to take 10 seconds to give you an answer to a search. Whether or not it is acceptable for a person to take 10 seconds, 10 minutes, 10 hours, 10 days, or 10 weeks to give you an answer will depend on the context. Because people are not machines. And we must demand immediacy from machines, not from people. People need time to stop, see, understand and act. Empathize with the context of the other. Give meaning to things in our life. That pressure to deliver immediacy as if we were machines is making us think that we are machines. We need time to feel, we are emotional beings and emotions are made to be expressed. If we bury them, the only thing that comes out is anxiety. Stress depression is the disease of the 21st century.

We live in the age of lack of focus. Not only do we have to deliver fast, but we have to deliver a lot of things. And they all demand immediacy. What keeps us busy and concerns us at work is added to what keeps us busy and concerns us in personal life, making our day-to-day a real production and delivery factory (and, of course, consumption). The problem is that our brain does not know how to *multitask* like the microprocessor of an iPhone. If a parent is taking their children to school late in the morning, while answering to an email from last night to his boss, while thinking about having a meeting with a customer in the afternoon, it is most likely that he won't do well none of those tasks. Think about the last time you had a conversation of more than an hour with a person in which neither of you was interrupted by his mobile phone, checked it nor, simply, kept an eye on it "just in case." If we live constantly (pre)occupied of what may occur, we are never occupied with what is happening, the here and now, which is the only time that really exists. In such a situation, how can we be happy? The problem of lack of attention goes, if I may say so, beyond happiness itself. Attention is the basis of awareness, which in turn is the basis of learning and knowledge. Out of the thousands of stimuli per second that our brain receives, attention is the ability that allows us to select those on which intelligence will act, acquiring awareness (realizing) that this stimulus exists and having the possibility of *taking it*: learning it, knowing it. If we do not pay full attention to what we are doing here and now, we are not fully aware of it and our cognitive system, our learning and our knowledge are diminished. Even for that "professional", "leader" (in big quotation marks) who has given up on his personal happiness, this lack of focus and attention is absolutely incongruous: who would trust, in the 21st century, a leader who is incapable of learning? We need conscious leaders. We need to get back the basis of learning and knowledge, consciousness. And for that we need to retrain our mind to pay full attention. In his book *Mindfulness: a path of personal development*, Santiago Segovia, Doctor in Psychology and creator of the *Mindfulness Based Mental Balance* (MBMB) program, calls this state of conscious leadership *"mindful* consciousness", as opposed to the state of "ordinary consciousness" that dominated by distorted automatisms, he is unable to focus with full attention to be aware of reality and learn from it.

We live in the age of lack of purpose. I came to this conclusion a long time ago, observing and trying to understand the context of the world in which we live from day to day. If we do not have time to do many things, and the things we do daily we do without focus, it is very difficult, not to say impossible, for us to have a long-term purpose, a WHAT FOR in our life.

I use WHAT FOR instead of WHY (which would be the natural use of the Golden Circle's WHY by Simon Sinek) on the recommendation of Curro Duarte, executive coach, who says that in Spanish, the question WHY generates rebound, looking back and excuse:

- "Why do you get up every morning?"

- "Because I have to go to work to make a living."

However, the question WHAT FOR generates reflection and projection for the future:

- "What do you get up every morning for?"

- "To make the world a more human place. And you, why do you get up every morning?"

While "going to work" or "making a living" are WHATs, "making the world a more human place" is a WHAT FOR, a purpose, a motivation that drives us from within stronger than any external motivation and allows us to lead ourselves and inspire others, helping to define the significant WHATs that will materialize our WHAT FOR.

Is it possible to lead a team or group of people without a purpose? Antoine de Saint-Exupéry said, "If you want to build a ship, don't start by looking for wood, cutting boards or distributing the work. First, evoke in men and women the yearning for the free and wide sea."

And, is it possible to lead oneself without a purpose? I think this is a very good question to be asked, without getting into whether one has or does not have a purpose nor what it is, if it had any. We will explore that later in the journey. I think that one must wonder whether it is possible to lead oneself without purpose. The answer for me is a resounding NO, and my point is very simple. The best synonym for the word leading is directing. That is, to give direction. In which direction do you point if you don't have a polar star to guide you?

What is really devastating is that I have been observing for years and I see many lost teams, who do not know if they are looking for wood for a ship or a bonfire, who do not know if they cut boards for a ship or a weapon, who work on the WHATs of a project but they do not know WHAT this project was designed FOR. And I see many "leaders" without a WHAT FOR, without a purpose, without a polar star with which to inspire themselves and inspire others.

People who roam day by day, week by week, year by year, through their lives, as if at some point, an angel was to go down from heaven to get them out of that routine that is their life and elevate them to the place where they believe that they should be by divine justice. People who talk about what they are passionate about in life in terms of a constant future, as if a sudden change was about to come, like someone who like someone who flops a straight flush in a new hand of poker, which would allow them to win the game. Individuals who live their life with the only mantra of *being set for life* (splendid incongruity) as if, after this life, they had another one in which to be fulfilled, enjoy and be happy.

In my view, lack of purpose is both cause and consequence of many years killing the behaviors that make us essentially human. Emotion.

Sensitivity. Vulnerability. Curiosity. Creativity. Intuition. And many others such as humility, empathy, generosity or the helpful attitude, that put others as catalysts of one's happiness, However, we have been led, educated and tutored in other values:

A concealedly blatant focus on tasks, processes and results at the expense of people.

An attitude of constant competition towards colleagues, collaborators and the team, fostering individualism rather than real collaboration that can take a team much further than what individual members can achieve separetely.

The banal pressure to show a profile of ongoing success.

An implicit consensus to penalize those who are shown authentic, natural, without artificial masks, sensitive, vulnerable, open and predisposed to failure.

An acceptance, by default and without too much critical thinking, of the fact that what is correct is what the majority approves.

A law not written nor spoken, that who prioritizes the care of his family self-imposes a ceiling for professional growth.

A false de facto purpose when "leading", which is the very fact of maintaining power and continuing to "lead."

As seen before, I think that the historical context has hugely benefited this trend. But I also believe that those leaders who decided to be brave, row upstream and fight for more human values in this so industrial context that was the middle of the 20th century, stood out back then and continue to stand out today because of their leadership style. María Montessori for her defense of an educational model based on individual talent, creativity and the use of games in order to promote the child's freedom of thought, a model radically in controversy with the educational system established at the time. Martin

Luther King for his fight for equality in diversity. Steve Jobs and his determination to break the *status quo*. John Lennon and his activism for peace. Margaret Thatcher for her implicit struggle against the dictatorship of male leadership. Mahatma Gandhi for his fidelity to the dictates of conscience and his non-violent communication.

Back then, you had to be a rebel to lead from human values. Today, the context has changed so drastically that I believe that this leadership style that for decades has turned its back on such human aspects such as conscience, emotion or creativity, has simply expired. And with him, those people who still preserve it.

Those people give name to this chapter. I invite you to observe and recognize them from now on. The leader of the 20th century is everywhere, like a *zombie* in times of apocalypse. On the street. In the subway. In the Steering Committees. In the schools. In the Governments. In the media.

Regrettably, many of those people have been our leaders over the past few decades and continue to be today. Their style of "leadership" is responsible for the fact that in the heads of many of us there is a mistrust in the very term *leadership* and in the system that, for decades, has nursed that style of "leadership", which in this context is more ally of control than of inspiration.

But the leader of the 20th century has achieved something far more important than generating that mistrust; it has rekindled the unrest of the restless, it has loaded them with compelling reasons to know that something structural has to change, and he has given them the impetus and energy so that each one finds their own leadership, more authentic, more conscious, more creative, more generous, more sustainable, that can contribute to transform this reality, for a greater, more human collective purpose.

Chapter 5

We have been educated to choose.

Why this severe lack of purpose even today, in the leadership of the 21st century? Reflecting on this, I met Caroline Ladousse, entrepreneur and coach, creator of the *Jobfulness* method, which helps people discover their talents and living off them.

She asked me about my story and I told her that a few years ago I left a large company in which I worked for years, to work in a much smaller company, from which I left after a year to start working on my own, on what I was passionate about and that currently, on top of this, I join as an intrapreneur companies and projects in which I believe. Then, Caroline said to me, "You're a *slasher!*"

I did some research and realized that the French are very good at naming market trends (in addition to being somewhat risky, due to the most basic aception of the term *slasher*), among other things because this makes that trend have a brand identity that can help in promoting the own dissemination of the trend. The so-called Pygmalion effect.

The fact is that *slashers*, Caroline told me, are those people who work on their own as well as on behalf of others, who have several projects at the same time, who have their own project and collaborate in that of others. At first, I thought, "lifelong moonlighters". But then I realized the power of this concept and trend in the present context.

Slashers are people who do not want to choose (hence the term *slasher,* which comes from *slash,* the denomination of the symbol '/' in English, separator for the various dedications or epigraphs with which a *slasher* would describe himself). The question a *slasher* asks when he is offered a position is not "what salary or rank am I going to have in this company?" but "how does this project and this company fit in with my purpose and values, with my core project?", and "how much time will I have to work on other initiatives that are part of my project?". The thought of a *slasher* is not "I have my own company, I don't want to know anything about working for others", but "in this other project, I could do the same thing that I do on my own and also learn and validate in another country or sector or with another scale of customers."

Slashers maximize the possibilities. In a world where everything changes abruptly and constantly, having open fronts means possibilities. And the possibilities are opportunities for connection, for those who know how to take advantage of them.

However, we have been educated to choose. Since we are children, we are choosing. Science or Arts. Pure or mixed. Choose a university degree. Choose a major. Choose. Choose in the most pejorative sense that implies a decision that closes the rest of the doors forever. Even more serious when we have to make those decisions with very little information, very little qualified; about a limited and pre-designed set of alternatives for mass education and therefore ignores the individual, his passions and talents.

I invite you to think about the real reasons why you chose a branch, or degree, or major. I will tell you mine to illustrate where I want to go:

At the age of 13, I liked Maths and I was good at it, so I chose Science (to keep studying Maths).

When I was 15 years old, I was terrified of studying Biology the way I was taught by my teacher at that time, therefore, I chose Pure Science, fleeing Mixed Science that included Biology (to end that ordeal).

When I was 17, I met the grade requirements to do Telecommunications Engineering and my mother told me that it was in fashion and had many professional opportunities, so I chose *Teleco* as a degree.

At the age of 20, I liked to program and it seemed to me that the world of computers and the internet had more for me than understanding the electronics of circuits or antenna networks. I therefore chose Telematics as my major.

However, nobody cared (neither did I then) everything that interested me in each of those moments and everything that I was giving up with each of those decisions:

When I was 13 years old, I was attracted to literature, poetry, and I was reasonably good at writing.

When I was 15 years old, I found out that I liked art and that painting in your style, with the proportions and colors that seemed good to you and without necessarily having any real meaning (sorry for taking this small license in the exacerbated description), had a hole in the history of art called Cubism.

At the age of 17, I adored sports, I liked to observe professionals or *amateurs*, I was good at practicing it and I liked training others.

At the age of 20, I loved music, had passionately studied the history of music and listened to music of all kinds, along with taking my first steps on the acoustic guitar and drums (and, of course, the *Hohner* flute! I will always wonder who delegated the responsibility of generating a taste for music in thousands of children to this diabolical and assonance instrument).

And far less mattered what I was good at but had no place in *the pre-established paths*:

I used to assimilate the emotions and feelings of others in the first person, which allowed me to empathize with other children easily.

I was good at imitating accents and tones of voice, even in other languages, with a certain grace.

I had a certain sense of intuition regarding the things that could occur around the groups of people with whom I lived on a daily basis.

In light of the moderately open jobs or challenges that the teacher asked of us, usually the student was the one to come up with a creative approach, different from the rest of the class.

Empathy, emotion, intuition, grace, sense of humor, creativity. These are still called *soft skills* today, a sort of aptitude complement to a curriculum of training, certificates and experience (the *hard skills*) that continues to be the fundamental part of a professional profile for the majority of the companies, the reason why decisions are made to hire or promote people.

However, if we look back, history tells us that technology has progressively stepped in for people in all the specialized professions to which we have devoted ourselves, and that the creative intelligence of people has been the one that has directed this evolution towards new activities in which the *soft skills* are increasingly critical.

Why no one told me then, "continue along this formative path, you must not lose that ability to empathize with the emotions of others?" or, "in this branch of studies, you will work and make that genuine creativity grow?" The system simply was not ready. The system, which needed engineers and lawyers, knew of science and arts. And you had to choose between science and arts. At the most it came up with was to recommend Architecture if you had good spatial vision. But creativity? Empathy? Sense of humor? Forget it.

I am talking about two or three decades ago and it may seem that the overall picture has changed a lot since then. But unfortunately, it is not like that. The current educational system is still very similar the one back then. Everything is oriented towards choosing from the existing options. And, no matter how much effort creative schools make in fostering multiple intelligences and individual talents in the early years of children's education, secondary education and access to college lurk with their gate of choice and selection. Some of those children will recall those *soft skills* as adults. Many others won't. The problem is that in two or three decades they may not be able to lose so many years of creative, empathic and emotional thinking, since Artificial Intelligence will be a very tough competitor in the access and performance of any job.

As an adult, I have realized that I did not want to choose between Pythagoras and Gongora, because I am passionate about writing about technological evolution. Or between my talent for science and human emotions because I love researching how scientific evolution can help people to get to know each other better and be more human. And thanks to the fact that in my memory I have stored those passions as a child, I have been able to connect them and exploit them as an adult. In a sense, I did not choose completely. And thanks to that, I have designed my own path, one that has to do with what I believe in and what I am passionate about. A path that did not exist between the choices that they made me make, that they make us all make. But for which I firmly believe that we have to fight. Because technology evolves quickly and automates specific skills, so we need people with human skills, capable of interrelating disciplines. And because, without passions and without individual talents, I believe that having a clear purpose is a task as impossible as it is necessary for the leader of the 21st century.

Chapter 6

Unlearn.

We hear that in this age of constant change and revolution, the only reason we will remain competitive is our ability and speed of learning. We hear that, to train our learning, we must *learn to learn*. It sounds beautiful, but where do we start?

I asked myself this question a long time ago and, after much observation of teams and people, I reached a conclusion: our own mental barriers are the reason why our learning mechanism is stagnated. There is no greater challenge than teaching those who do not want to learn.

Therefore, the question led me to another. Why do we stop learning? It is clear that we know how to learn. We have been doing it our entire life and we keep doing it. However, we do not do it with the speed, intensity or depth that the current context demands of us, and we have the feeling of not reaching it. At some point, we stop learning in the most essential sense of the word: learning to know more. And then, the question is: do we really want (have the right attitude to) learn? Or do we prioritize other factors such as the return that investment in learning will have in our professional careers? Mental barriers.

Unlearn. What a beautiful and challenging word at the same time. On the one hand, it seems a simple thing (if I have learned something, I can forget it, *unlearn it*). On the other hand, it contains a huge difficulty for it to be a meaningful action. We are not talking about forgetting the little things that do not add value to our life. Our brain takes care of this alone. We are talking about disassembling models, paradigms, mental structures that we have rooted in our head, conditioning the way in which our brain processes new information, and that are simply no longer valid today. This now gives more vertigo.

However, it is more necessary than ever. And I will take examples from the business world to visualize this need:

In a context in which American and European citizens would not care if 92% of brands disappeared tomorrow (*Meaningful Brands* study by Havas Digital), it is obvious that those businesses are doing something wrong.

In an environment in which the number 1 talent retention factor is alignment with the vision and the sharing of values between company and employee (as stated by Spanish human resources managers to Infojobs), but in which at the same time 38% of workers at global level do not feel that their personal values are aligned with the values of the company they work for (according *to State of Employee Engagement*), there is something wrong with those cultures.

In a world in which 94% of Generation Z believe that brands should take action against social and environmental problems (according to a study by Cone Communication), it is worth wondering how many companies have their Director of Sustainability or Corporate Social Responsibility in the Steering Committee, or how many of them have in their strategic plans as a company the UN Sustainable Development Goals in which their business can cause a greater impact.

All these dilemmas appear when the structures with which we have designed a system (in this case, the company) keep functioning the same despite the fact that the context has changed, sometimes radically. But the thing is that we live in a context in which change is the only constant. What do we need to adapt faster to the context? How can we prepare our mind for that constant learning that the new environment demands of us?

Unlearning implies a different attitude before the context that surrounds us. An attitude that is:

More courageous. Forget about stability. Embrace change.

More open. Forget about the profile of continuous success and the fear of failure. Welcome mistakes and learnings.

More generous and collaborative. Forget about protecting what you think belongs to you. Enjoy frugality.

More attentive and curious. Forget about the path you are supposed to travel. Contemplate the possibilities.

Humbler and more creative. Forget that you already know. Eternal apprentices are sought, who learn by doing and who learn quickly.

More conscious and meaningful. Forget what they have taught you. Get to know yourself and understand what you can offer to the world.

In short, a more human attitude.

In the unlearning, the journey begins. A journey that you must do in the first person, counting only on your attitude. It is not little. In fact, it is all it takes to move the world, attitude.

Unlearning is just the beginning of the journey. Arming yourself with all these attitudes to begin to face reality will soon begin to provoke different actions, results and situations, never seen before. But do we by any chance learn from what we have seen before?

Chapter 7

Attitude Pact.

At the beginning of projects, workshops and even any meeting that I facilitate, I always suggest this attitude pact to the teams that I collaborate with. It is an action guide that each participant arranges with himself and with the rest of the team and it remains agreed from the beginning of the project. It is the backpack that will come along on the journey, and to which we will draw on when there are moments of weakness, doubt or conflict. I recommend that you prepare it with love and keep it yourself as well throughout this journey.

Divergence

Take a blank sheet of paper and draw the following.

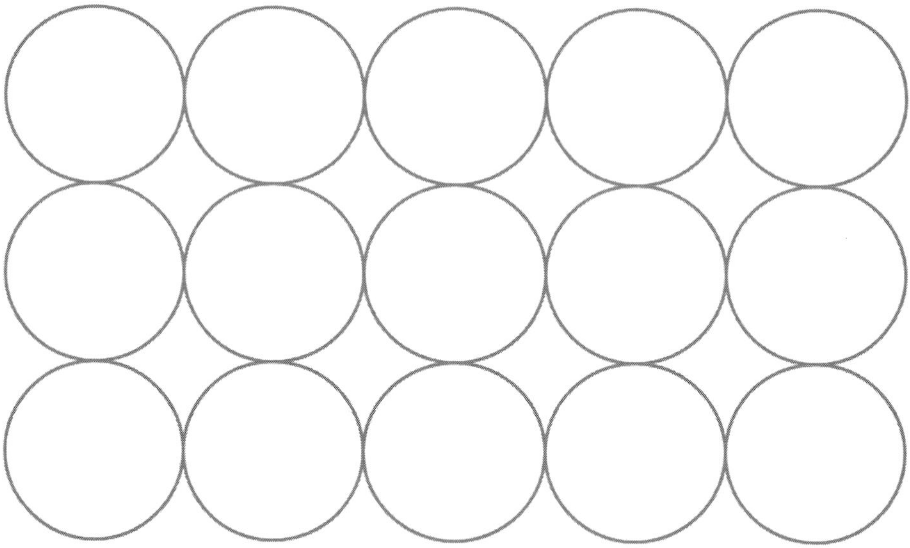

Take a marker and a stopwatch.

When you read the following instruction, start the stopwatch and stop it only when you have finished the task. Ready?

Write, as fast as you can, something round in each of the circles. Go ahead!

Go with the flow. It's part of the attitude pact, just do it!

Are you done?

Was it hard to complete all 15 circles? How long has it taken you to do it?

The fastest ones take about 30 seconds. Impossible? Look what they wrote.

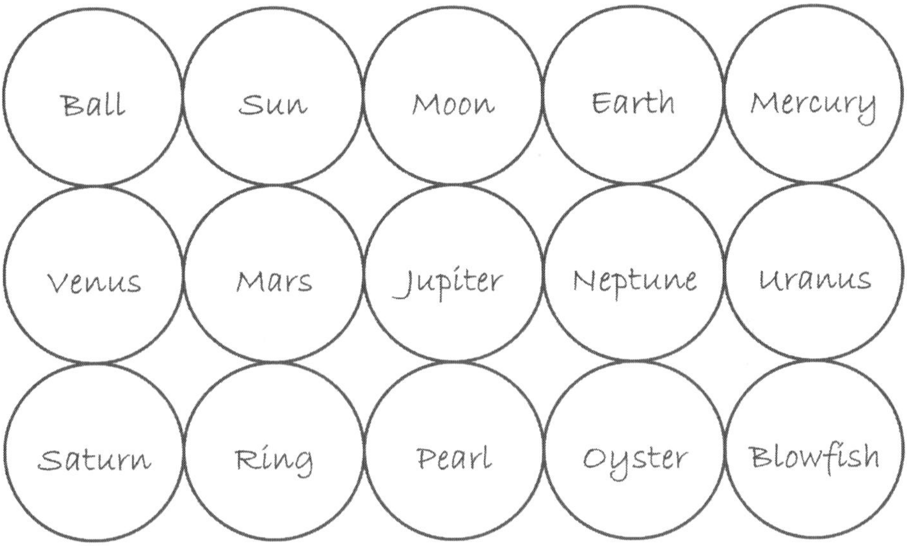

You may have written Earth. Why haven't you written all the planets? You would have advanced 9 circles very fast. Not only that, but maybe, when writing Saturn, you would have come up with ring, which is also round. And when writing ring, think of pearl. And of pearl, oyster. And of oyster, blowfish. All of them round.

In the description of the task it was only indicated to write something round in each of the circles, and as quickly as possible. Nothing was said about whether writing 9 items from the same category (planets) was correct or not. Nothing was said about subcategories either, so with one of the first ideas you probably had, ball, you could have done the same thing: tennis ball, basketball ball, football ball, paddleball, volleyball ball, handball ball, etc.

This is an example of how sometimes our mental structures force us to carry out actions conditioned by certain patterns, even making us forget something as clear as the problem formulation (which we can compare with a customer's brief).

The interesting thing about this dynamic is not the fact of going faster when writing repetitive ideas or of the same category, but the capacity that these ideas have to generate new ideas, in oneself or in others. In the context of a certain project, the ideas "ring", "pearl" or "oyster" may not make much sense. But perhaps "blowfish" is the idea that helps us focus the project. Therefore, the way to get to generate this idea was worth it.

I call this dynamic Divergence because that is how divergent thinking works. Generation of ideas with no more restrictions than those enumerated in the framework of the problem, without worrying about whether they are good or bad, astute or stupid, new or repetitive, only seeking to generate the largest volume of ideas possible in the shortest space of time and trigger divergent thinking in oneself and in the rest of the team. Intellectual autonomy and critical thinking are two components of divergent thinking that boost creativity.

Divergence is the first element of the Attitude Pact to travel this journey. Store it well in your backpack.

Constructive Feedback

Our brain grows drawing maps (hence mind maps). From an idea that it draws in the center, it grows with ideas that are branching to the outside, as if it was a tree, which makes its way through its branches and sub-branches.

When there is a non-constructive judgment facing an idea that our brain generates, the growth path of that idea is cut off and the brain becomes blocked.

Every divergence process is associated with a convergence (in the previous example, they would be the evaluation criteria that led us to decide that "blowfish" was the idea that could help us focus the project). Therefore, all feedback that we are going to give to our own ideas or the ones from the team (I include myself in your team), must be constructive feedback, which allows to continue growing, building on it. Try these structures to give feedback:

"I like that idea because..."

"That idea triggers another, which is..."

"Perhaps, by picking up that idea we could do..."

"I liked it when you said... and in the future I would like to see more..."

Instead of non-constructive structures of the type:

"That is very difficult to implement."

"That is very expensive."

"That was already tried years ago and did not go well."

You might have heard these last sentences at some point. As they highlight, they do not build and therefore kill creative mental activity.

If you remember, Artificial Intelligence worked in a very similar way: drawing trees and exploring its branches to maximize the learning that it draws from each of them. The important thing is not to find only the best ideas (or avoid the bad ones), but to maximize learning. Let us not put up barriers to the development of our own intelligence. Constructive feedback, second element of the Attitude Pact. To the backpack.

Play

Play is the most natural and universal vehicle for human connection. We were all children and we played, with the only purpose of playing because by doing it we had fun, we created new worlds, it made us happy. A pure purpose, without any barriers and meaningful, don't you think?

As adults, sometimes, playing makes us feel uncomfortable, wanting to give up thinking that we have made a mistake ("I'm old for this", "it is nonsense"). Do not succumb to that first impulse, let out the child that we all carry inside and that invites us to be explorers and curious.

Playing and learning are two words that dance together in harmony. They release the creativity that is natural in all of us, just like when we were children. They amuse us.

Enjoying ourselves makes us happy and that is a nice purpose. Play, to the backpack.

Rebound

How high does a tennis ball bounce when you throw it on the ground? The answer is "it depends on the strength you pull it with."

It is the same on this journey. The more you put in of yourself, the more you will take. Do not wait to read the solutions to the challenges posed in this book. There are no more written solutions because only you know the solutions to your challenges.

Take a blank notebook, post-its, markers, your best predisposition and to the backpack.

Players and team

The Boston Celtics surely ring a bell with you. Do you remember anything this team did? Something big, unique. Something in the 60s.

The Celtics of the 60s won eleven champion rings between 1957 and 1969, eight of them in a row, something that no other team has ever achieved in NBA history.

Could you name a player from those wonderful Celtics of the 60's? (No, Larry Bird is from the 80s). Exactly. Me neither. The greatest feat in the history of the NBA and we do not remember any star of that team. The star was the team. All and each one of its members and the style of play that they developed as a team.

Another good example would be our fantastic Spanish football world champion team in 2010. Iniesta, Villa, Casillas, Cesc, Xavi, Silva, Busquets, Ramos, Pujol… it is impossible just to keep a single star. As a team, invincible.

The success of a team project depends on what each of its members puts of themselves and that they, together as a team, add up more than each separately.

Players and team, to the backpack.

Full Attention

The past is immutable and the future is uncertain. The only thing that exists is the present, the here and now, and our choice as beings is to be or not to be in that present. If we are, we can do and learn, knowing, being aware and paying full attention.

Train to be in your present, be it having a conversation, reading a book, going on a trip, participating in a workshop or meeting, or playing with your children.

Full attention or *mindfulness* is the basis of consciousness and learning. Full Attention, sixth and last aspect of the Attitude Pact, to the backpack.

Divergence. Constructive feedback. Play. Rebound. Players and team. Full Attention. This is the Attitude Pact that you sign now, with yourself. Store it well in your backpack, the journey is long and there are curves ahead. We will need to turn to it.

Part II.

Master your ego and your fears.

Diverse seemingly impossible tasks that the hero must overcome. It has faults and different degrees of illumination. Discover powers and dangers.

Chapter 8

Titulitis aguda.

Do you remember that feeling you had when you were *nothing*? Don't get me wrong. When you were not in possession of any title that would certify you as an architect, teacher, mechanic, doctor, engineer, MBA, etc. You were hungry to get it. You were striving to learn. With the necessary ambition to reach that goal you set for yourself, but with the humility of someone who knows that he has not achieved anything yet.

You did it. Secondary Studies. Vocational training. Bachelor's degree. And maybe even a master's degree. You beat those levels and got your degrees. And these opened the doors of that company or that position from which you could make a living.

And then what? Hunger was switched off. I won't be so unfair. Every two or three years you pay for a course that you complete with great effort and fattens the list of titles on your resume. What do you do that for? The correlation between that course and the long-awaited promotion in your company is zero.

I am sorry for the extra dose of critical thinking (forewarned is forearmed), but this is the sad reality of the system in which we live. The educational system is so stagnant that it continues to function based on titles and certifications, as if that was the reason that can differentiate you from another candidate for a promotion, a job or, in general, for the execution of any activity that generates a value. And we have become used to these rules of the game in such a way that we suffer from *titulitis aguda*[1] and are prisoners of our own ambition and competitiveness.

Let us put that ambition and competitiveness to work for us, positively. Let us do it with a practical example that I am addressing to you and in which I am going to make many assumptions based on what I would feel and do if I put myself in your shoes in the example.

Imagine you are offered to give a TED talk next month about, say, Intrapreneurship. You will get on a stage in front of thousands of people and talk for 20 minutes about something that you do not consider yourself an expert. The video of your presentation will certainly be posted *a posteriori* on www.ted.com, where it will be subtitled and viewed by millions of people around the world.

Have your arteries already frozen in fear? Since you have read the word "scenario", you are not thinking about the opportunity that giving this talk could entail, but about the panic you have to go on stage, how little you could tell about Intrapreneurship and the world-wide ridicule you can do if something goes wrong (which will indeed - you think-).

After that minute of initial blood blockage, you get a rush of confidence and adrenaline and you accept.

You have a month. One month to do whatever you want, you can think of and you can in order to prepare your 20 minutes TED talk on Intrapreneurship and make it a success.

You start by googling "Intrapreneurship." Hundreds of references and cases about Intrapreneurship before you. You see words like innovate, open new lines of business, or work differently within an established company. You evaluate to what extent what you have done and are doing in your company is Intrapreneurship. Cold sweats. You keep reading.

---

[1] Excessive valuation of titles, academic degrees and certificates as a guarantee of someone's knowledge.

You try the same search on Linkedin and you find a former colleague of yours from the company where you worked a few years ago who recounts how his years working in that company were a nice case of Intrapreneurship. "He has a nerve!" - You think at first. When delving into it, you realize that what your former partner says makes sense and that the only thing he is doing better than you is telling it, somehow, selling it. You decide that you can do that too and you start writing an article on Medium telling your story as an intrapreneur. Thousands of doubts assail you when you write it, but you do not give up, you investigate on Google until you answer them and finish your article. Bravo.

What has happened? A real external motivation has made you mobilize. The commitment acquired after the rush of confidence and adrenaline for the very opportunity that giving a TED talk can imply, has been the impulse of an ambition that, in turn, has awakened a curiosity and a concern that have made you do something (write an article on intrapreneurship), from which you have learned.

You have learned. That is the essence of education. To learn. Not a title. And it must be accompanied by motivation. And only you can find what motivates you and put it right in front of you as a goal to achieve.

After a week with your article on Medium published and shared on Linkedin, you receive 50 recommendations and 15 comments congratulating you. Not just because of the article itself and the story it tells, but for the fact that you have been brave and exposed yourself, shared your own story openly and honestly with others so that others can learn from it too. And that triggers you new lines of thought. "If my story has helped others, I can organize a *Meetup* and set up a small workshop to apply these learnings to other companies, even other sectors". And you organize it. And 6 people attend, but you put the same affection as if 60 had attended. And not only do they learn and you learn from your own history, but they learn and you learn from the history of others. And you rehearse and improve your presentation and your *pitch*. And one of the assistants invites you to join a WhatsApp group of people with whom he shared a creativity workshop the previous year and they get interested in your Intrapreneurship workshop. And you present it for 60 people. And suddenly you say: "I wish I had the opportunity to get on stage to give a TED talk about Intrapreneurship." Bravo.

Bravo, not for the talk, which was something invented and that at this moment we could take out of the equation. You could not give that TED talk, but you already have a value to add to those 60 people about Intrapreneurship. Bravo for the path of motivation, curiosity, learning and action that you have undertaken thanks to it. Now the motivation comes from within with much more force. Projecting our motivations into the future calls us to action. And action is one of the basic principles of creativity and learning. Move and you will learn.

Elon Musk, famous leader of project initiatives such as Tesla or *SpaceX*, aims at connecting the human brain to a machine. And if Elon Musk has contemplated something, we have compelling reasons to declare that it will happen sooner than later. Think that when this happens, all the existing knowledge on the Internet will be accessible for anyone, at any time, instantly and naturally, as if that knowledge was stored in our minds by -for example- having studied it.

"It's not about what you know, but about how quickly you learn", says Lucas García, one of the greatest references in Digital Marketing in Spain and with whom I had the privilege of working. The speed at which you learn will be your differentiation in the age of Artificial Intelligence. And for that you need to stay motivated, curious, active. It is a bit romantic but do it for the love of learning - that is the very essence of learning. Not a title or a certification.

A person's worth is not determined by his university degree. In 2013, Lazslo Bock (Google's *Chief Human Resources Officer*) said that they had realized that the correlation between a person's academic record and his good or bad performance in the company was zero. Some of his teams already had already more than 14% of members without any university degree functioning perfectly within the culture of the American internet giant, and the tendency of that proportion is growing. "Unless it is a person who has just graduated from University" – Bock says - "We will not look at whether or not a candidate has a university degree".

To play a good role in a company like Google, which leads change in our era on an ongoing basis, you need curiosity, the ability to approach and investigate problems whose solution is not obvious, and know how to learn. And that, in the vast majority of cases, they have not taught us at University. Sadly, it is often the opposite: concrete answers are sought, not multiple solutions and good approaches.

There is a reality. Degrees do not guarantee an attitude of continuous exploration and learning, highly demanded by companies and people in the context we live in today. But there are also good news. It is possible to awaken that attitude.

Chapter 9

Collaboration or competition?

In the movie *Heaven Can Wait*, directed and starring Warren Beatty in 1978, Joe Pendleton is the captain of a famous American football team, which is preparing to play the *Superbowl*. In a scene at the beginning of the film, a journalist asks him if he is worried about the early recovery of his rival, Tom Jarrett, since he could reach the final. To which Pendleton responds with a profound and sincere face of astonishment: "Jarrett is not my rival, he is a partner! My rivals are the other teams."

I have always loved this movie and in particular this scene, which is no more than a plain and ordinary scene from a plain and ordinary movie. However, the face of absolute astonishment with which the protagonist stands for something so obvious as collaboration between colleagues from the same team is, seems to me the most authentic thing. The journalist, with his question, represents the most simplistic reality: the fact that only one *quarterback* can play the final and that this will be Pendleton or it will be Jarrett. Nevertheless, Pendleton ignores this simplistic reality, does not even give it the slightest importance, and replies to the journalist with another greater and deeper reality: the fact that he and Jarrett are partners and that whoever plays the final, they both share a common goal, which is to win it.

Have you ever stopped to think how much of *Joe Pendleton* and how much of a *journalist* there is in our day-to-day behavior? I have been observing work teams for a long time and unfortunately, I see many more *journalists* than *Joe Pendleton.*

We have been educated to think this way. Selective access tests, selection processes, selective promotions. The whole educational-labor system is designed to put us in competition between us, since the selection of a candidate necessarily implies that another or others will be rejected. The team collaboration so longed for in companies and work teams remains as mere words on a wall or *Powerpoint* if real decisions are made by competition among individuals.

Not only that, but the labor market constantly encourages us to differentiate ourselves from each other and this, somehow, makes us close ourselves off, not share, not collaborate. *"Nos esse quasi nanos gigantum humeris insidentes"* ("We are like dwarfs on the shoulders of giants") said Bernardo de Chartres in the 12th century, referring to the fact that a single person has a limited range of vision and understanding, but supported in others (in this case, *giants*, knowledge accumulated throughout History, in the knowledge of others), his vision and understanding are broader, not because he has greater visual acuity than the others but, precisely, because of his greater height when supported in others. But this, in the competitive market, does not differentiate us, does not justify our salary, does not help us compete.

How much it limits us to think like this. It makes our mind consider the system in which it operates as a separate sub-reality, in which the goal is to compete and win within that sub-reality. Winning the *Superbowl* (winning a contest, winning a customer, renewing that customer, obtaining his recognition) becomes a secondary goal, an instrument at the service of particular interests of individuals within the organization, which the organization itself has fostered. These insterests are closing and end up understanding the resources of the organization as individual rights (*their* position, *their* bonus, *their* promotion, *their* team, *their* budget, *their* right to severance pay) in an absolutely alienated way. Individuals put the protection of what they consider *theirs* before the belief in a greater purpose, the real collaboration to achieve collective goals and the pride of belonging to the group.

Of course, this is never obvious. We always find the inauthentic collaboration in the form. And at the bottom, the real competition among individuals. What is actually at this bottom is the essence of any organization, its culture. And when the culture in which an organization operates is that of competition among individuals, collaborations are never authentic but just another mere instrument concerned to serve individual goals.

Inauthentic relationships. How much of this is there in our day to day? Authenticity is the reason we humans trust each other. Trust is the basis of all relationships, both between people and between organizations, as well as between organizations and people (be these customers, shareholders, employees, the press, *partners*, society or, in general, anyone who has any relationship with the company and therefore an opinion about it. Lack of authenticity is something that an organizational culture and its members simply cannot afford.

The same thing happens with people. We enter the economy of trust. Our reputation, both in the real world and in the digital world (whose border is increasingly blurred) says it all about us, and this is determined by our collaborations, the trust we have generated in them. Share or protect? Open or closed? Contribute or extract value? For a collective purpose or for my personal interest? Collaboration or competition? In the digital age, there is no longer a place for *wolves in sheep's clothing*. These are decisions that any leader must make and be consistent with day after day.

By prioritizing competition over collaboration, we can win in the short term, but we will be sacrificing the medium-long term because we have risked our authenticity. I think we simply cannot afford this. In the long term, there is always the generous and authentic purpose and the leaders who have been able to overcome the simplistic reality that makes us compete with each other, collaborating with each other for a greater and common goal that makes us greater as a team. *Win the championship.*

Chapter 10

The double edge of humility.

Humility is for me, by all means, one of the qualities that any good leader must have.

However, it is a tricky skill. The Aristotelian principle applies especially to humility: *virtue is in the middle way*. We can think that this happens with all abilities, and it is true. But I think that with humility it happens in a more marked way than with other skills, since both extremes of humility are especially dangerous.

Lack of humility can lead us to not listen, not empathize, and not accept *feedback* from others. Without humility, we lose a significant proportion of the exploratory spirit that ignorance awakens. If we are not able to admit that we do not know, it is difficult to be curious and ask questions to know. Falling in love with our ideas just because they are ours can lead to unreason and isolation.

Many leaders of what we have called *the 20th century* err on the side of lack of humility because they confuse leading with having power. The lack of humility of a boss with his team because he is the boss generates frustration and kills creativity in the team, which is already serious. However, it creates an even more dangerous effect on that person: lack of self-criticism and dependence on power to influence.

At the other end, the excess of humility also creates counterproductive effects. *Humble is selfish* says Pablo Álvarez, a leader focused on Innovation and Strategic Design in the field of talent and corporate culture, referring to the excess of humility that, curiously, can unleash exactly the same effects as lack of humility: unreason and isolation. Although for different reasons.

The excess of humility can cause a lack of autonomy and critical thinking to challenge the ideas presented by the reality in which we live. Thinking that we do not know or are not sufficiently legitimized to express an opinion on an issue that affects us, can lead us to accept the approaches of others without any questioning, which is nothing but a mental derangement that generates dependence on others.

The overly hierarchical structures with which our society still operates encourage this to happen. It is a challenge for a person to maintain a solid argument in which she firmly believes before another person who argues the opposite if this other person is her boss. We tend to think of it as a challenge. We are afraid *to be contrary to the boss,* and we end up giving him our intelligence away and being mere executors of instructions in sequence, (you remember the definition of algorithm, right?).

The motivation for someone to adopt this behavior of excess of humility is not necessarily a humble personality driven by shyness. It may also be due to an excessive fear of losing our position and our economic livelihood. Or, to an excessive comfort in the face of the problems that reality presents us, aware that *someone else will come to solve them,* not without a certain selfishness as Pablo underlined.

As obvious as it may seem, we do not realize that, in the 21st century, people do not receive their salary for not thinking but precisely for doing it. For contributing diverse, critical, informed perspectives. And for making debate a virtue, diversity of opinions a cultural asset and joint argumentation a more solid approach.

In the middle way is virtue, and especially with humility.

Not knowing a topic does not imply being unable to lead its exploration, from the acceptance of the ignorance. Being in charge of a team, project or initiative does not mean being unable to show vulnerability to the uncertainty and challenges in front of that team. This generates empathy in the team, which sees that the leader is not a demigod to whom power grants reason, but one more of the team, who is next to the team and who has the ability to ask questions from the ignorance and initiative of search for answers to lead the way.

Nowadays, anyone with access to the Internet, the ability to ask the right questions and an exploratory spirit can acquire a reasonable knowledge of pretty much any subject in a relatively fast way. Not accepting that is as ridiculous as thinking that a boss knows more by the fact that he is the boss.

The environments that reality presents us are complex. Humility is undoubtedly a virtue with which a leader can show acceptance, curiosity, generate empathy, find solutions in such environments. Without conformity. But above all, without egos.

Chapter 11

You only have one life left.

Do you remember when playing a video game or playoffs as a child, you only had one life left? Or when your team was losing by a goal and there were only a few minutes left until the game was over? Do you remember what you used to do? You gave it your all.

Pepe Martín, entrepreneur, creator of *Minimalism*, blogger and author of *El creativo encerrado*, has a different and radical way of expressing this in real life, which I like very much because it causes shock and reaction, as obvious as it may seem, "you are going to die". And so it is. Until some Silicon Valley scientist proves the opposite (everything today is under the umbrella of possibility), we are all going to die, we have an expiration date.

Pepe's motto, which gives the title to his blog, is #muerevacio (www.muerevacio.es). And it is basically about that, giving everything while you are alive. Because in life there are no green mushrooms, no *insert coin*, no other round, no new season. You only have one life left. How you live it is up to you.

Over the course of my life, many people (friends, acquaintances, even people who do not know me at all) have told me a phrase: "you live very well." It is a phrase that, for some reason, we tend to take on the negative side

(I include myself because I did as well for some time). The "what's the matter, don't you work?" side or something similar.

But if we look at it on the bright side, the phrase "you live very well" is probably the best thing they can say to you. "Of course! I have a life and I live it well. Much better than living it badly! I'm glad you see it too."

There is a certain sense of irony in both comments, the observation and the replica. The simplistic reality beneath the observation is a feeling of envy that the replica tries to ignore. Envy is human and therefore understandable; we all envy someone for something at some stage. The key is how we handle this feeling of envy.

It can be a blinding envy, which makes us react with an irrational feeling of rejection towards the envied person because, somehow, it represents what we would like to be, but we are not, or something that we do not know or that scares us and therefore we reject.

Or we can dominate that envy so that it does not blind us or silence some of the many questions that we would probably ask that person. "How do you get to work 6 hours a day? How do you do to travel so much? Where do you get so many business opportunities? How do you know a certain person? How have you managed to always work from home and not miss a minute of your children's lives?" Again, the questions, that magnificent and powerful tool that few use enough and very few use well.

Humility also plays here. Knowing and accepting what things you do not know but yearn for, or what things scare you but you need to face, and therefore you must ask and investigate in order to transform your reality.

I go further. The equanimous control of our emotions, whether we label them as *good* or *bad*, leads us to ask ourselves questions of a greater impact. "Why am I envious when I talk to this person? What does she have that I would like to have? Why don't I have it? What would I have to do to have it? Why do I feel rejection for what comes from this person? Is it something that I would like to do but I do not dare? Why don't I dare to do it? What would I have to do to dare?"

And I go even further: if you don't dare to make the decisions of your life, who is going to do it? And if you don't do it in this life, when are you going to do it?

It is exactly the same with work. In a company, there are only two types of workers: those who have already been fired and those who are going to be fired. It is a bit of an extreme way of saying that everything in life has an expiration date. At work too. But, for some reason, we tend to think that the jobs, the positions, the projects are infinite. And that sometimes makes us lose perspective and delay or totally ignore some of the vital choices that are calling us from within strongly.

I have a proposition for you:

Take a sheet of paper and write down the 10 things that you like doing the most in life and that you do with a certain regularity (whatever).

Now, take another sheet of paper, write down the 10 things you would most like to do in life but have never done before.

Now take another sheet of paper and write the numbers from 1 to 10 one below the other.

Remember the attitude pact. Do. Play. Generate bounce. The difference between just thinking of these lists and making them can be abysmal. Stop for a moment, think, and write your lists.

The 10 things on the first page are your fulfilled passions: you know them, you fulfill them (and you surely enjoy them, congratulations!).

The 10 things on the second page are your unfulfilled passions: you know them, but you do not fulfill them and therefore they are an unfulfilled dream. The question that your subconscious throws at you is: when? "When am I going to fulfill these passions?"

The 10 things on the third page are your hidden passions: you do not know them, therefore, you do not fulfill them, you do not dream or enjoy them. The question that your subconscious throws at you is: what? "What is there beyond what I know today? What if my greatest passions were yet to be discovered?"

There are people whose second page is the same as the third: it is empty, they do not have unrealized passions because they do everything that they are passionate about. And they frequently "fill in" the third sheet and update the first, exploring and discovering new passions. One might think that these people are lucky and/or rich. However, their pattern has nothing to do with luck or money. In fact, they do not usually believe in luck but in the discipline of overcoming and often make money arise as a consequence of their courage to pursue their passions (we will talk about this later).

Their common pattern has to do with the absence of a bond that other people do have: fear. These people live without fear, aware that they only have one life left and that only they are responsible for what to do with it.

It can give us vertigo. It can generate envy. It can cause us fear. We can take a fourth page and write the 10 reasons why we cannot live like this. But the real question is: what is scarier, to live fulfilling your passions or to die without having done it?

Chapter 12

Regaining control: money cannot be an end.

Let us start from a consensus: we all need money to live. Those are the rules of the society we live in, and if we live in society, we must comply with the rules.

I want to establish that starting point to prevent the reflections in this chapter from falling into the *naif*. Above all, after we have encouraged ourselves in the previous chapter (I deliberately drag you into this) to live the passions of your life to the fullest and wildly.

I also like to start from this consensus because we have a certain tendency to think that there are things in life in which others are luckier than we are. Money is one of them. And I would like to make this chapter useful to anyone, no matter what their financial situation is.

Having established that lower where we have agreed that we all need money to live, I want to explore what the upper limit is.

What is your financial goal in life?

I do not know if you have considered it, but it seems to me an interesting and necessary *sanity check*. Try to give a numerical answer to that question. Do not be content with a "the more, the better", that mentality only fuels the block.

Take any sheet of paper, one of those invoice envelopes that you keep receiving from your water supplier, and let's keep asking ourselves questions:

What average salary will I earn *(P)* throughout my life? Here you can speculate all you want. But try to be realistic. Look at the evolution of your salary in the professional years that you have and project. Do not think that it will always go up. You are a product that a company buys and compensates, and as such, you have competition. From other humans or, increasingly, from machines that will do it more efficiently and at a lower cost than you will. Sometimes you will have to accept salary cuts, new lower paid jobs or stages without income. Oh, and I would take the net (I would not count on our taxes being returned the day we no longer work).

A curve like the one in the graph could be a good guide.

Calculate by eye the average wage of this curve by drawing a line at a height *(P)* so that the sum of areas a and c is approximately equal to area b.

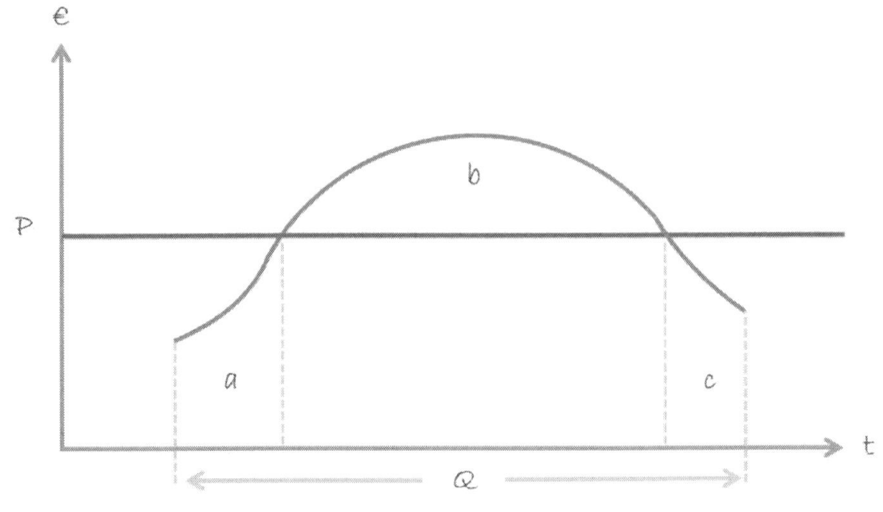

How many years am I going to work *(Q)*? The answer will depend on how old you are, if you are closer than far from retirement, maybe around 40 years old. If you are further than close to retirement, by observing a little the trends in retirement age, longevity of people and the emptying of the public pension system, you will know that it is more conservative to think that you are going to work most likely for 50 years.

Multiply *P x Q* and you have it. All the money you are going to earn in your life. Exciting, isn't it? I am not saying it because of the number (which will be whatever it is), but because you can already say that you have done some *back-of-the-envelope numbers.* I also say that it is all the money that you are going to earn in your life without taking into account any other income, asset, heritage that has not entered into these calculations, although you can always enter it. What I do not count on is the case of the 0.0001667% mathematical probability that you have that you win the National Lottery. I still find people who live keeping an eye on that percentage to pursue their dreams (perhaps in *another life*).

Now that you have that figure in your power - all the money you are going to earn in your life - you have a new power in your hands. Being able to accept what things you will be able to buy in life and, more importantly, wich ones you won't. And since you know that neither by salary nor by chance that you will win the Lottery you will be able to buy those things (and live that life that those things mean in your mind), you have in your hand, right now, great potential. You have the option to accept it, and let it go.

Difficult, isn't it? We do not want to forget that fantasy in which we live a better life than the one we have today, thanks to the fact that at some point "fate (or the Lottery) will put us in our place." It is an easier thought than accepting reality. But you just did the numbers. And they do add up in order to lead that other life. Or maybe it is that our head has not wanted to accept the numbers?

Life is like sailing on a boat. If a captain leaves Ibiza for Cabo de Palos, he has to set course from the moment he leaves, and maintain it throughout the whole journey. Foreseeing the wind and current and weathering any possible unforeseen on the route. If he just leaves, he puts on the *automatic pilot,* have a Gin Tonic at sunset with its east wind and after a while, he checks where to enter the port, he better call Denia or Alicante, because Cabo de Palos is no longer going to make it. If you wanted to buy that house, or that boat, maybe you should have started working before, or in something else, or studied another degree, or you should have not studied at all and have dedicated yourself to your passion since the age of 7. Perhaps. But probably, with the current course, you will not make it, and those plans are nothing more than a utopia that are preventing you from accepting and fulfilling what your real passions are.

Let us think about that for a moment. We are born. We grow. We work. We earn money. We spend money. We die. With no goals, no passions, no dreams, and most importantly, no purpose that guides all that, life is a journey on *automatic pilot* that reduces itself into that sad sequence. And there is a trick in that sequence. An infinite loop. Earn money - spend money. The more I earn, the more I spend. The more I spend, the more I need to earn. And I can keep doing so all my life.

Of course, we do not say it like that. That loop takes different forms. A car. A bigger car. A house. A bigger house. A house on the beach. A bigger beach house. A boat. A bigger boat. Form of small material goals for which we need money, for which we need to forget about our passions and keep earning it.

In his book *Rich dad, poor dad,* Robert T. Kiyosaki calls this loop *The Rat Race,* as it is like a rat running and trying to escape from a wheel that keeps turning, without making any progress. The longer the rat runs, the faster the wheel turns.

The reality is that we live like this, and we do not realize it. And that's where the real problem lies, in not realizing it, in living in *auto* mode. Because that is the moment when money has become an end in itself. Which actually does not make any sense, since money is something that represents another thing that has a value. That is why we people invented money, to be a manageable, comparable and universal element for the exchange of goods that do have real value (they can be used to make something), such as wheat (eat), a sheep (extract wool) or a piece of land (live on it).

Therefore, if money does not have a value in itself (tell that to countries with annual inflation above 20% such as Argentina or Venezuela) it does not make any sense that it is an end. And far less a purpose. What is behind *The Rat Race* is ambition. I am not saying it is wrong. What I am saying is that ambition as a purpose does not make sense either (why do you want a bigger house? There is no meaning and there is no purpose if the answer ends up being "to have a bigger house"). Ambition as a means of achieving a meaningful and helpful goal is a great skill (for example, being ambitious and opting to win a championship, award, or contest from a customer, or successfully executing a project that will improve the lives of people). But ambition as an end, like money, are linked to the human ego, and they do not make sense.

We are clear that we do not want money for the fact of having more. But we have said that we were going to flee from the *naif* moment. And the reality is that we need money to live. That takes us back to the infinite loop, to the rat race. How to get out?

The answer has to do with creativity, with awakening creative intelligence and regaining control of the ship you command. And for that you must know where you are going and, more importantly, what guides you. Your pole star. Your purpose.

But first, a penultimate stop.

Chapter 13

What will they think of me?

- "But, what are you going to live on?"

- "All of that is very nice, but real life is another thing."

- "Let's see if you learn how to do business in the real world."

- "Once you jump, there is no turning back."

- "That's all fine, but it won't pay your salary at the end of the month."

These are some of the famous phrases that one hears when he has found his purpose and has understood that he must start his own path to live it day by day, despite the fact that it involves painful and risky sacrifices.

The first challenges come in the form of advice from those that surround you. From the affection, but also from the inevitable protection and from their own barriers. They are the first proof that your finding is significant and authentic. In my experience, it is more difficult to convince a mother of a decision such as leaving everything to pursue your dreams, than to convince a customer that you can be the best ally for his business, even if you have just started.

The doubts and challenges that arise at the beginning of the journey are the natural human reaction to any change, even if it is only a project: denial. The closest environment reacts with the most pessimistic hypotheses almost spontaneously.

Take advantage of those questions. Listen to them and think about them in depth. Look for the answers. Do not question the essence of the journey (living your purpose) but improve the way in which you are going to undertake the journey.

The logical reaction to this natural denial is to look at yourself in the eyes of others and think, "I'm making a fool of myself." "What will they think of me, if I have not started yet and I already have doubts about myself?" Remember the attitude pact: *constructive feedback*. Take advantage of the *feedback* of others to complement your vision, but do not overwrite it, make it stronger. The others are not you, they cannot see with your eyes, feel with your heart. It is not the time to seek external acceptance, but internal acceptance, that of self-knowledge. Remember: the mind needs to understand reality to survive and transform it in order to be happy. We are still understanding reality, that of oneself. Transforming it through others comes later.

Doubts are not the end of the road, but a crucial part of it. Do not let them bring you down. Take advantage of them to make yourself stronger.

Chapter 14

Write your epitaph.

I discovered my purpose by talking to my grandfather. I do not remember a specific day but rather a succession of days when I used to go to see him, sit, and talk to him on his couch. He would tell me little things about his life and I would listen to them stunned, so immersed in the story that I forgot everything else. As if there was nothing around and there was nothing else in the world. Like when you are reading a book and its content or an idea inspires you in such a way that suddenly you see everything clear, easy, to the point that, at that moment, you feel that you could organize your reality perfectly around that idea and everything makes sense. Like when you live an experience in such an immersive way that, when remembering it, you do not need to describe the sensations that you had when living it because, that simply does not matter, and you focus on the purity of the facts.

My grandfather was a calm person, who could be listening to you talk for hours about something that was serious or complicated for you and that, just by his way of listening and being, ended up transmitting his serenity to you and made that problem practically fade away. He also knew how to give good advice and many people turned to him for his practical advice that he gave from the lucidity of his serenity and from his great listening. He made things easy: not because he simplified them, but because he was a very intelligent person, deeply spiritual and he knew how to separate the wheat from the chaff, keep the essentials. He was a person who had his own light and who illuminated with his example because he did not do things for himself but out of pure love, out of pure kindness and generosity towards others, to give the best to others, without filtering it with his own benefit. That was his happiness and his light.

I remember that he showed me his drawings with drawing pens from when he was studying, he told me about his first job at *Renfe*, he told me about his numerous jobs and how he was always thinking of new projects in which to give the best he had to improve the life of his six children and all those around him. And he talked to me about my grandmother, he talked to me a lot about my grandmother whom he loved with all his heart and he did so over the course of his life, putting her first and giving her everything.

I was watching him, sitting on his couch, telling all those stories of effort, passion and generosity to his grandson, and I realized that it just made him happy. Because I also felt that happiness. That feeling of happiness that being present gave me, listening to him calmly and without worries or distractions (serenity), with a deep sense of the essential (lucidity) and without any filters, judgments nor responsiveness (equanimity) helped me to discover something very important.

When my grandfather was no longer there to tell me more stories, I understood that he was happy giving, making others happy. And that, by telling me those stories, he was fulfilling a dream. Over time, I understood that my grandfather was a great leader, because his great love for others made him give, inspire others and encourage them to achieve goals for the common good, greater than himself. That is how all of us who knew him remember him.

When I saw my grandfather above and inside, I understood that my purpose was to continue with his life of search, effort, passion, love and generosity to be a leader for others, inspire them, encourage them to find their essence and live it day by day, to make this world a closer, calmer, more human place. And maybe one day, to be able to sit on the couch with my grandson and tell him those stories.

That is my purpose. That is my pole star and my guide. And every step that I take on that path every day, my happiness.

Expert sailors say that sailing is not just about knowing the sea, the wind and your boat, but to navigate you have to know where you are going, and for that you have to know where you come from.

It is not easy for a person to understand her purpose. But when I understood mine, thanks to the last talks with my grandfather, I noticed a very relevant question that could help others in this endeavor.

This is the last question, the last tool of this stage of the journey. And it is deep, so I will suggest that you make a a stop on the way before continuing, to think it through. At this stage, we have understood that ego, competition, double-edged humility, comfort, envy, fear, ambition, money, or doubts are nothing more than mental barriers that prevent us from understanding our purpose, understanding what we are in this world for, realizing our passions and living who we really are to lead giving the best of ourselves.

When you are no longer in this world there will be none of these barriers. The tool is called *Write your epitaph*. The question is: What do you want to be remembered for? That is your purpose.

Intermission.

A stop on the way.

The hero discovers how vast and powerful love and unconditional dedication are. The hero faces and is initiated before who holds the greatest power in his life. The culminating moment of preparation.

We have reached the middle of the journey and I want to invite you to stop to breathe in and understand where we are, before continuing.

In this first part of the journey, we have analyzed the current context in which we live with constant change and evolution and we have understood that a leader can no longer be without a conscious and personal purpose, without being a leader of himself before leading others. We have grounded this context to the individual situations that may be blocking us from day to day. Finally, we have begun to become aware in the first person, to understand our purpose in life, why we would like to be remembered once we are no longer here.

Those day-to-day blocks, usually egos and fears, are what prevent us from walking the path guided by our purpose; that is, to be leaders of our own life, to live the life we want to live, since only then can we be an authentic example to lead others.

I invite you to revisit at this moment the three questions that I asked you in the *Intro* of this book:

Would you take the job you are passionate about for half the salary?

Moreover, would you take the job that you are passionate about without receiving any salary at all?

What's more, would you work without any salary to make what you are passionate about a future job?

Have your answers changed? Has the determination with which you answer these questions changed? Has the way you view these questions changed?

When I reached this point in my journey, I had a feeling of freedom similar to when I was a child and had no ties. It was like being reborn. I did not know what I was going to do, but I did know what for. And suddenly I saw everything differently. I was clear about my purpose, now it was *just* a matter of finding what I could live with day by day, the WHATs that would build my path of my WHAT FOR.

In that search, I had a big help. It was something that also emerged, as did the purpose, after reconnecting with myself, the fruit of self-knowledge, which connected me with that sensation of full, serene, lucid, equanimous awareness of the conversations with my grandfather. A backpack with several items that I gave you before your journey of self-knowledge and that I hope has inspired you.

Finding that backpack for me meant arming myself with my basic acting principles, my values:

Restlessness, exploration, curiosity (Divergence).

Do not judge the opinions of others (Acceptance).

Play and seek fun by maximizing learning (Play).

Give the best of myself before expecting to receive (Rebound).

Find and surround myself with people with whom to collaborate as a team that seeks a collective goal greater than the individual one (Players and team).

Maintain a *mindful* awareness (serenity, lucidity and equanimity or non-reactivity) that reminds me WHAT FOR I do the things that I do, through the feeling of happiness that my grandfather transmitted to me (Full Attention).

Those are my HOWs, my values. The filters with which I evaluate if my actions and the way in which I execute them add up to my purpose or not.

I invite you to benefit yourself from that backpack that has accompanied you from the beginning of the journey and fill it now with your own values, your principles of action for whatever you do. Values (HOW) provide the glue, the discipline necessary to find congruence between purpose (WHAT FOR) and day-to-day action (WHAT).

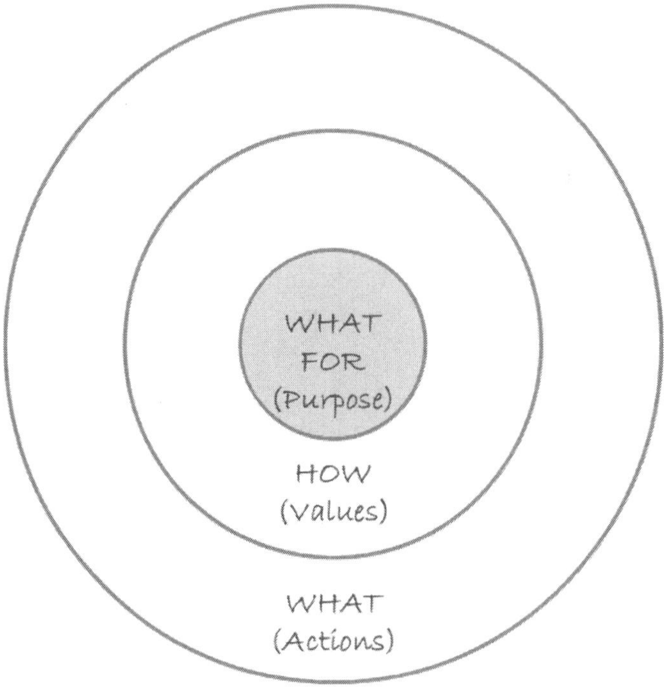

Inspired by the Golden Circle, by Simon Sinek.

Part III.

Release your natural creativity.

The final metamorphosis or transformation elevates the hero to a higher plane and a parenthesis of calm and plenitude ensues, preparing the climax. All the previous steps helped to prepare the hero for this moment in which he achieves that precious transcendental goal.

Chapter 15

Creative Renaissance.

I admire children. I believe that adults should observe and listen more to children and pay more attention to what they transmit to us. With their curiosity, sincerity, activity, energy, imagination and purity, they are little teachers of life and many times, we do not even realize it.

"Why?" When a child does not know, he asks. He has no need to pretend that he knows something that he does not know, and naturally identifies people or aspects of the environment that can provide information about it. He investigates. He explores. He asks and asks to infinity, he does not get tired, he does not put barriers to his curiosity. And he learns.

"You know what?" When a child knows something, he does not keep it quiet, he shares it with everyone, he is transparent, he is sincere, he tells stories.

When we give a child a blank sheet, he imagines and creates. Try asking a child to draw something and then tell you about it. It is astonishing to see how, at 2 or 3 years old, children's creations, absolutely abstract, perfectly connect in their minds with the story they want to tell us. And how as they grow, the creations and stories take forms that adjust more to reality.

When we become adults, reality is in charge of teaching us the border between the real and the imaginary, the right or the wrong, even the socially appropriate or inappropriate. Somehow, we leave behind the behaviors that shaped our natural creativity. As noted by José Antonio Marina and Eva Marina in their book *El aprendizaje de la creatividad (The learning of creativity)*, these behaviors are: "Activity versus stillness. Expressiveness versus muteness. Innovation versus repetition. Discovery of possibilities versus acquired impotence syndrome. Opening versus closing. Critical independence versus intellectual submission. Autonomy versus dependency." We can observe these behaviors in children when they are curious and ask why. When they are brave and let go of their parents' hand to walk alone. When they make up stories. When they tell them. Every day.

We define creativity as the ability to generate new ideas or concepts that produce original value solutions to real problems. We find two well-differentiated parts in this definition: generating new ideas or concepts and producing original value solutions to real problems.

In contrast to what many think, creativity is not only the generation of ideas, but it is also the channeling of those ideas to produce original value solutions to real problems. Creativity brings together the world of imagination (that of ideas and, if you allow me, the world of children), with the world of reality (that of problems and solutions, the world of adults). In any creative process, these two phases are tackled in a clear and differentiated way: divergence (generation of ideas without restrictions) and convergence (selection of the best ideas according to the parameters that contextualize a problem).

However, the context in which we live today makes us be much more in the world of reality, that of problems and solutions, the world of adults. And we do not have time to imagine, to devise, to generate new or different ideas that can add the "originals" attribute to those solutions.

In the adult world, we see restrictions, problems, urgencies, and blocks before possibilities. So we tend to systematically solve problems in a linear way, going for the first thought that comes to mind, the one that guarantees us greater security against failure, the one that assures us that we are not going to be labeled *crazy* for thinking different from the majority, settling for the most *cliché* thinking. Exploring possibilities is a crucial part of creativity that we can observe and must learn from children. They also have a much more natural acceptance of emotions that help them explore and create, because they do not judge them and, therefore, do not repress them.

In the executive world, having a bad day, having fun or feeling certain emotions, is often something that the context makes us hide behind an artificial mask, as if emotions, what defines us as humans were not *serious* (it is enough to consider if one wants to be *serious* or human, right?)

And it is as if those emotions that we feel as human beings were not precisely what makes us explore, create and think in a different, unique way. How many times have we heard company managers ask their employees to think *out of the box* (that is, outside the parameters of the known or conventional)? My question for them would be: what have you done to encourage your employees to think *out of the box*? If that *offsite* that companies do once a year creates a context that turns out to be so positive for the team, each individual, the collaborations, the laughter, the personal complicity, the motivation, the culture and consequently the business, why don't they replicate it more? This type of environment brings out the best of each person because we relax, we do not repress our emotions, we feel freer, more ourselves. A little bit like children, at heart. It is no coincidence that the game is one of the most used resources in this type of executive dynamics. However, this seems reserved for one *motivational* event per year. The rest of the year, we must return to our *adult self* and manage our jobs in a *serious* way, acting in a *serious* way and thinking in a *serious* way.

We have forgotten about the child we all have inside. The one who asked "why?" The one who said what he thought. The one who felt and expressed. The one who imagined, painted and told a genuine story starting from a blank sheet. And with that, we have forgotten an essential part of creativity: creating. Create alternative paths when the solution is not obvious or the context is complex. Create new possibilities by the simple fact of having been brave and gone out to explore, when the safest or most comfortable thing would have been to design a theoretically direct path. We want to think *out of the box*, but the need to generate certainty, the pressure for short-term results, and the demand for immediate responses make us think more linearly than ever, in a more uncertain context than ever.

Paying full attention to the children, I realized something else, a master lesson from those little great teachers of life that they are: when a child plays, he does it for the sake of playing, because it makes him happy. Is there a purer purpose than this? Can there be greater congruence between what one would like to do and what one actually does?

As we become adults, reality, context, society and ourselves, make us separate our purpose from our everyday life. That there is no congruence between what we would like to do and what we do. That our life becomes a routine of production and consumption of what others indicate us.

If we look at History, Renaissances always arose to bring the human being back to the center of our own lives, after stages of something else, be it Theocentrism until the Renaissance of the 15th century or what I consider a too industrial approach to work seen from the beginning of the 19th century and personified even today through the leader of the 20th century.

I came to the conclusion that releasing the creativity that we all had when we were children and that channels our essence as human beings is the great discovery to unlock the human leadership that the era we live in today needs. Creating frees us from executing in sequence, in *auto* mode. Creating embodies our authenticity. Creativity makes us shine unique.

Creative Renaissance. Creative reawakening. That is what this part of the journey is about.

Where to start? Start, literally, with what you like the most: activate your passions.

Chapter 16

Activate your passions.

Let us rescue the three sheets of chapter 11. Those in which you listed your fulfilled passions, your unfulfilled passions and the blank sheet that represents the hidden passions.

Complete the second list, the one of unfulfilled passions. Now that we have traveled to the past, to when we were children and we did things just for the sake of doing them, remember what you liked to do the most back then. When you were a child, a teenager, younger. Think about what fulfilled you, your hobbies, your *hobbies*, little things that made you happy.

Add the things that make you happy today.

Now, let us remember one of the principles of creativity in children: their activity, their energy. There is no creativity without action, because there are no good original ideas if they do not solve a problem, if they do not generate a transforming action. Therefore, I am going to suggest you start by taking action. Some ideas:

Google your passions. Find out what is being done today.

Contact, through social networks, people who are today involved in one of those passions.

Find an event related to those passions near you and sign up! Meet in person people who reconnect you with your passions, engage in conversation beyond the event.

Search on Linkedin about your passions, identify people who also share them, follow them, write about them. Read them, interact with their content, follow them, contact them, ask them to go grab a coffee and meet each other!

Write down new ideas that you come up with doing all of these things (activity calls activity).

When I facilitate individual and team sessions, for this part, I lean on the Passions, Talents and Opportunities map. I invite you to use it too since it is a very simple visual tool that can help you discover and progress with your passions until you even make them a way of life.

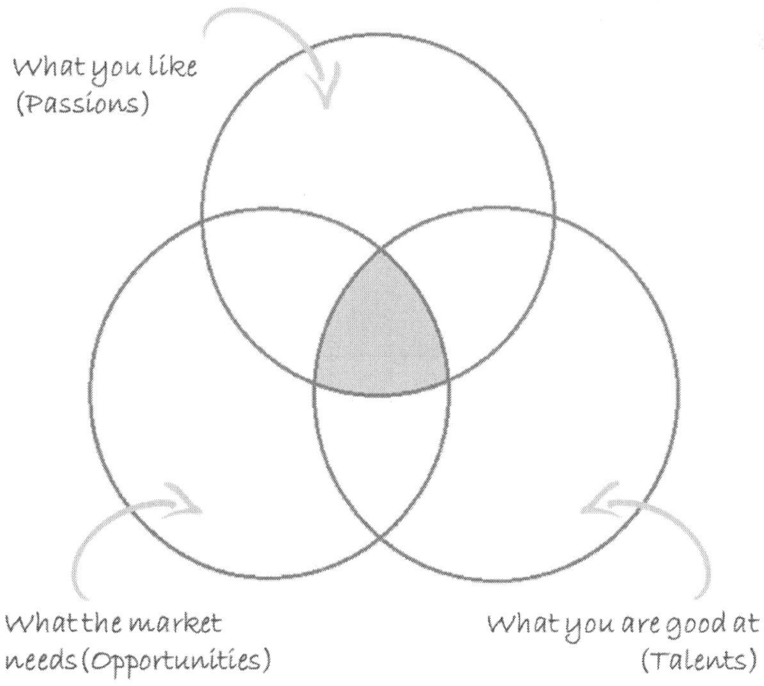

One thing that works very well with visual tools like this one is to hang it on the wall and use it as something alive. Take advantage of your activity to feed the map (put a post-it for each item on the list of passions you made). Think about which of those passions are also talents (that is, you are good at them) and move those post-its to the intersection area between Passions and Talents.

Take advantage of your activity to discover opportunities: from searches you do, events you attend, people you know, conversations you have. Investigate. See what other people who are dedicated to those passions you share are doing and identify opportunities ("what the market needs") that you could fill.

Also, take advantage of the map to generate new ideas of activities that you could do and do it. The goal is to identify one or two ideas that are in the central area, where your Passions, Talents and Opportunities converge.

Ken Robinson calls this area *The Element*. Japanese culture has a similar concept called *Ikigai* that distinguishes "what the world needs" and "what you can earn money for" within the opportunities. I use this simplified map and make it independent of the fact that you can earn money or not, since, in my experience to identify and generate value in an authentic, essential way, at the beginning you have to forget about money and it always appears later, as consequence of the value created. I call the central zone essence, where Passions, Talents and Opportunities converge.

This tool has served me on many occasions to help people and teams to materialize their purpose in a concrete action plan to start with. I believe that each person should aspire to find their essence, and act to live from it to have a fuller and more directed life. If we think about that competition to which we are all subjected, I think it makes much more sense to think that each person is unique because of the essence that defines his own passions, talents and opportunities, than to think that people should differentiate themselves by obtaining titles, obtaining *masters* and collecting impersonal career achievements.

Finding the WHATs that materialize the WHAT FOR helps to achieve consistency on a daily basis that allows us to first lead ourselves and then lead others thanks to our own example. It is difficult for me to think of the head of a team that today tries to inspire leading from the comfort of his position and his salary without congruence with his personal purpose, without being able to authentically demonstrate that he is passionate about his job and without consciously choosing to be there day after day.

To begin by discovering and activating one's passions is to ignite the spark of a flame that moves us from within much stronger than any external stimulus, be it titles, positions, success, money or power. It is to awaken an entrepreneurial attitude that we all have inside, crying out for a more congruent and authentic life. To some extent, I believe that we are all entrepreneurs since we all have a responsibility to lead the great project of our own life.

We will get there, but first we will take advantage of that spark that passions have ignited, to recover another forgotten behavior of childhood that will help us maintain and expand the flame: continuous learning.

Chapter 17

Expand your comfort zone.

We continually hear about the comfort zone. I have personally heard (and used, I must admit) the expression "getting out of the comfort zone" hundreds of times in the last few years. "You have to get out of your comfort zone" (motivational introduction to team dynamics). "To think differently, you have to get out of your comfort zone" (personal counselling to an executive in the process of professional reinvention).

A person's comfort zone is that fictional area that represents all aspects of reality that this person is comfortable with. Sounds good. Humans are beings of habits and customs. We get to any place and we engage with the reality of that place until we make it our own and feel comfortable in it. I think anyone in his right mind would choose to be comfortable over being uncomfortable. Why this eagerness to get out of this area then?

The human mind, as we said at the beginning of this book, needs to understand reality to survive and transform it to be happy. We are active beings. Our brain expands feeding on new experiences of which it wants to be an active part to produce valuable solutions that transform the reality that surrounds it. And that makes us feel alive.

Curiosity is the skill that prompts us to begin this exploration. From starting new projects in unknown fields, traveling, meeting new people, to small details such as going to work by a different route than usual. All are mechanisms of exploration of our mind triggered by curiosity. We are all explorers to a greater or lesser extent.

What happens outside the comfort zone? Try to recreate the last time you did any of those *explorations*. The environment is chaotic, uncertain. We do not know where to start. We are lost. We feel uncomfortable. We are afraid. We have questions. We doubt that embarking on that adventure was a good idea. We want to go back to base. Sometimes we do. Other times we are humble and brave. We try hard. We get spirit and courage from where there seemed to be none. We are attentive. We ask questions. We try things, as crazy as they seem. We make mistakes. We learn. We relate aspects of the new reality with the one we have stored in our memory. Little by little, we understand this new reality and incorporate it into our mind as an experience.

Sometimes we communicate only with headlines and we lose the essence of the message we want to convey. Leaving the comfort zone is the first step, a curiosity impulse from our mind that wants to expand. A revulsive. And it is very necessary. But the learning journey does not end there, far from it. Let us not think that getting out of the comfort zone means that everything else will be already sorted.

The actions in the previous paragraph are examples of the paths any exploration can take, but it all depends on the person. For me the interesting thing is the whole journey. The one-way journey (leaving the comfort zone, recognizing the new reality, feeling lost, being afraid, wanting to give up, making an effort, asking, overcoming fear, discovering) and the return journey (being tenacious, overcoming barriers, understanding, relating, connecting, applying, learning, transforming, sharing with others, listening, asking again, improving). Has it ever happened to you that, after a time living abroad or a journey in totally transformative adventure mode for you, have you tried to share that experience with your environment, but you realize that "everything here remains the same"? You have changed, but your environment has not, nor does it want to, and your challenge now is to share your discoveries, your experience of transformation to also transform your reality. Transforming your reality is as important as the transformation that has previously occurred in you, because otherwise, the change is only valid in your mind and that leap with reality will tell you that something is not working, causing us frustration and pushing us repeatedly to get out of that reality. This exit is actually a flight of the mind and for me it is a dangerous state in which we can begin to build a parallel reality just because we have not been able to transform our reality, to complete the journey with what we learned outside of the comfort zone.

The discovery and transformation of oneself is as important as the action and transformation of the reality that surrounds us. In order to successfully execute this transformation, we have to share, communicate, collaborate, inspire, and thrill other people who are part of our reality, with the findings we have made in the new reality. We cannot change others, but we can change the relationship we have with others. With humility and empathy, but with vision, tenacity, conviction and gifts of meaningful and inspirational communication. Some call it leadership.

That is why I propose that we stop talking about "Leaving your comfort zone" and talk about "Expanding your comfort zone." We humans are beings of habits and customs. Getting out of your comfort zone is just the first step. No one can continuously live outside his comfort zone, his mind would go crazy. What is really interesting about this exploration journey are the mental mechanisms that we set in motion to discover the new reality, understand new concepts and create associations with the concepts that we already know of our base reality (our comfort zone), to expand it and feel comfortable in a new larger reality. Expanding our comfort zone is creating a new reality, it is discovering or creating new WHATs that can be part of our essence area, it is growing intellectually and it is one of the mechanisms of continuous learning that we long for and need in the context of constant and accelerated change that we live.

If successfully executing the one-way journey (leaving the comfort zone) was related to curiosity, to be successful on the return journey, the expansion of the comfort zone, we must master a universal human skill. So universal and so human in theory, that it might surprise that it is so highly valued in practice. But the context in which we live has made us take relearning it very seriously. We talk about communication.

Chapter 18

Communicate to thrill, from your essence.

We talked in the previous chapter about expanding our comfort zone through sharing our experiences with our environment to integrate and transform it.

Communication is one of the *soft skills* (or, as I prefer to call them, human skills) most sought after by companies at present. It is not surprising since communication is probably the most powerful tool of the human being. Everything we say, we do not say, we do, we do not do, we feel or we do not feel communicates. And when that communication manages to bring out emotions, it has immense potential.

Communication has the power to transform even oneself, the sender of the communication. If we have a cheerful expressiveness, we verbalize illusion, we gesture openly, we communicate positivity, and that makes the world about which we are communicating more positive in our own eyes. On the other hand, if we communicate negativity, fear, boredom, monotony, we will see the gray world.

Have you stopped to think about how your communication is on a daily basis? And about that of those around you? I have come across many people who communicate negativity. Some, although the minority, due to lack of attitude. The good thing is that these people are quickly identified, "I am negative, and I do not want to change." Just as quickly, we should get away from those people. However, in my experience, most cases of negativity are due more to a lack of self-awareness than a lack of attitude. When you do not know yourself, it is easy to project your fears outward, although the rebound effect is devastating. These types of people are more difficult to identify. They are usually negative, reserved or cautious in general, but in relaxed situations or when they are around more positive people, they tend to bring out the euphoria that they would like to keep up and cannot. I have met many people in this situation and the good news is that positive communication is a middle ground that is achieved by working it.

We have just rescued our own passions. Let us try starting there. Look at your communication when you talk about your passions: the words you use, your facial expression, your tone of voice, your gestures, your mood, your body expression, the brightness of your eyes. Ask others to help you understand what you transmit when you talk about what you like. That is the pattern that we have to try to achieve in our communication in general, regardless of the subject we are dealing with. Transmitting, bringing out emotions is a very powerful tool of communication.

Taking advantage of the journey of self-knowledge and discovery that we made in the first part, I will cite the recipe that Simon Sinek gives us to inspire others with our communication: *"Start with why"* (it begins with the WHY; or the WHAT FOR, as we said previously). "People don't buy what you do, they buy what you do it for." While most people focus on communicating facts, data, actions, great leaders communicate from the purpose (what they do things for), through their values (how they do it) to end in concrete actions (what they do). From inside the golden circle outwards. From self-knowledge to relationship with others.

I did the test myself in the process of writing this book. When I started writing it, I decided to tell it to a group of more or less trusted people and observe their reactions. I communicated it to half of them from the WHAT:

- "And what are you up to now?"

- "I am writing a book."

- "What about?", "Interesting", "Where do you find time?" - were some of the reactions with an interest, let's say, relative, more because of the unusual fact than because my communication turned out to be exciting.

To the other half, I communicated it from the WHAT FOR:

- "And what are you up to now?"

- "I have taken advantage of these transitional months to think and get to know myself better to know where I want to head towards from now on. Reconnecting with the conversations with my grandfather, I discovered that my purpose is to help other people lead in a more meaningful way and contribute to making the world a more human place. So I have resumed my vocation as a trainer and I am writing a book about it."

- "Awesome! I could not agree more, and how much that mentality is needed today! Let me know when it comes out"- was the majority response, accompanied by a face of deep emotion and some "goose bumps."

Every day we are telling stories. The face with which we say good morning to those who are closest to us. The mood with which we arrive at work. The little "thank you", "how are you?" or "congratulations" that we say, how we order or deliver things. The way we order our words to create a coherent and interesting thread. Empathy with the receiver. Choose the right time. Choose the right channel. The handling of silences. How we open and close the stories. How we connect stories and contexts. Attention to detail in our emails or our presentations.

Have you ever stopped to think what is special about the pieces of communication that have thrilled you, that have given you "goosebumps"? A talk, an article, a book, an advertisement, a song, an album, a movie, a concert. I invite you, when a piece of communication thrills you, to analyze it and extract its essence, some pattern that you can reuse in your own communication. For example, the thread of a film that navigates us through a classic narrative structure beginning - middle - end. Or an advertisement that uses silence and music to emphasize key moments. Or an album or a concert that opens and closes with the same verse or the same chords, like "closing the circle."

All of these are communication resources that can be worked on and trained. And they are important. As David Ogilvy said, "Tell the truth, but make it fascinating." In my particular adaptation of this magnificent phrase, I turned it around: "Communicate to thrill, from your essence." In other words, work and train your communication, use it to transmit and bring out emotions, but do not force it, always lean on who you are, what you do things for, your authentic *self*, your purpose. Authenticity and emotion in our communication to inspire and help others from our own example: that is human leadership.

The most important part of communication has been, is and will always be the message. Just like the *core* of the best marketing campaign is having an excellent product. You cannot transmit what you are not. Authenticity always comes to light. This is why, I propose that you overcome the fashion of the *storytelling* (which, like all fashions, will pass), and practice *storydoing*: that your actions tell your own story; the total congruence between saying and doing, between doing and being, between your actions and your purpose, between what you are passionate about, are good at and add value to others; be your essence and let it tell your story. The one for which tomorrow you will be remembered.

Good leaders know their purpose (they know WHAT they do things FOR, for what ultimate purpose), they know themselves (they know HOW they do them, how they are, what their values are, their principles of action), and in their everyday life they communicate that awareness of purpose and values through their actions and their words (WHAT they do, WHAT they say). They are natural leaders, because they create followers because of their authenticity and their ability to inspire and bring out emotions by doing and communicating what they believe in.

The connection that occurs between an inspiring leader and the people they inspire is an authentic, conscious, emotional, robust, sustainable and long-term connection.

In this part of the journey we have released the creativity that is natural in all of us, that connects us with our purpose and our passions and that great leaders use as a natural vehicle for inspiration and transformation of their environment. That connection that you, as a conscious creative leader, can create with other people is something much more powerful than any transactional relationship motivated by a useful product, a convenient price offer, a tactical *partnership* or any WHAT you can imagine. It is a great asset. Put it to work for you.

Chapter 19

Work for yourself.

In chapter 12, we talked about *The Rat Race* by Robert T. Kiyosaki, who explains us how most people are trapped in a loop between wanting to earn more to spend more and again needing to earn more.

At the end of that chapter, we said that the way out of this loop had to do with creativity, and we began a part of the journey that has to do with awakening that creativity that is natural in each one of us.

I would like to close this block with the exit of the loop. Not because I believe that everything begins and ends with money, far from it. But because I want this journey to be, in essence, a transformative one. And for that we must tackle all the aspects that make up our reality, including the economic one.

People who come out of *The Rat Race* follow a principle: "don't work to make money, make money work for you." The key to this principle is in the generation of assets that we have already mentioned several times. Let us look at it.

In financial terms, people who are trapped in the loop work only with the Profit and Loss Account. The more I earn the more I spend and the more I spend the more I need to earn. Earn income, spend costs. Probably in your personal or family finances, you are clear about the sources of income and monthly expenses. If not, I invite you to open an *excel* sheet and design it, at a high level (only the most important aspects). Something like this:

Profit and Loss Account

Income	**$1,960**
Payroll	$1,900
Parking space Rental	$60
Expenses	**$1,620**
Home rental	$1,000
Car payment	$150
Supplies and Internet	$150
Ben's school	$120
Food	$120
Go out	$80
Margin	**$340**

People who break the loop work with the Profit and Loss Account and the Balance Sheet. The Balance Sheet is the financial reflection of the Assets and Liabilities situation of any business at a given time. Reflect your personal balance on your sheet. An example:

Balance Sheet

Assets	**$33,000**	**Liabilities**	**$16,000**
Parking space	$15,000	Car debt	$7,000
Savings Account	$10,000	Parking space Debt	$9,000
Car	$8,000		
		Equity	**$17,000**

Assets being all that you have and Liabilities all that you owe, in economic terms and in a greatly simplified way.

Now consider for a moment that you are a company. That you or your family are a business. That you are your own product. Let us explore your current business model and potential opportunities.

What are the income lines? Divide them into Active Income and Passive Income, being:

Active Income: that income that necessarily imply your daily dedication. For example, your salary at work is active income.

Passive Income: that income that does not necessarily imply your daily dedication. For example, the monthly rent of an apartment or garage that you own.

In a purely financial sense, to generate active income, you work for money (the source of active income is your dedication, your job; for example, your salary). While, to generate passive income, the money works for you (the sources of passive income are the assets on your balance sheet; for example, the rental of the garage you own).

In the asset column on the balance sheet, we normally list properties (apartments, parking spaces, investment plans, shares, etc.). To have assets, we have had to invest previously. There are higher risk investments and lower risk investments, but we are always talking about money that generates money, without you necessarily having to work on it daily.

One can think then that if to get out of the loop you need money (to invest in assets and that these in turn generate passive income), this is actually another loop, since to earn that money you need to work. The trick is in your hand. You have already traveled the journey that has discovered your purpose, your passions, your creativity. What is missing *is just* to trust and invest in it, also financially.

Take the sheet where you completed the list of your passions in chapter 16, together with the table of your financial Balance. And now let's think: which of these passions are *per se* or can they turn into a financial asset? Don't think that only titles and properties are written in the asset column. Ask yourself "what if…?"

"What if I really started using those 500+ contacts that I have on Linkedin as an asset?"

"What if I spent the necessary time weekly to read about the topics that I love?"

"What if I started writing articles on those topics and posted them on Medium and Linkedin?"

"What if I created a website or blog on that subject that I am passionate about above all else and started forming a community of people with the same passion?"

"What if I organized regular *Meetups* with that community to discuss that topic and the community grew?"

"What if I looked for schools to teach on that subject?"

"What if I published a book on that subject?"

"What if through all this I got to know that great leader that I admire for her mastery of this subject?"

"What if tomorrow I became a landmark for my mastery of this subject?"

"What if I created a method for tackling complex problems related to this topic and patented it?"

Your network of contacts is an asset. Usually people think, "I need to work in my network of contacts, make it grow and strengthen it; but I do not have time." People who get out of the loop see their network of contacts as a virtual organization in which they are the CEO, and that brings mutual benefit to all members, regardless of where each one works. People who *work for themselves* invest time cultivating, growing and strengthening their network of contacts, because that way their network will work for them.

Any publication, article, podcast, web, blog, your own social media profiles that anyone in the world can reach at any time interested in something you have to tell, are assets. Normally people think, "I have to update my Linkedin profile" or "at some point I would like to open a personal website or blog where I can talk about my projects"; but they do not find time. People who *work for themselves* invest time developing digital assets that speak for them anytime, anywhere in the world. Think that your service, your work, is a product that you want to sell to someone who wants to buy it, whether in the form of a product that you have developed, a course that you facilitate or your own services as a consultant or as an employee of a company. Do not leave the sale of that product only in the hands of the *cold door* (for example, sending the CV to companies when you are looking for work). This is the worst sales channel in the digital age. Expose your value, what you can contribute, and let whoever is interested in your product do so proactively and without your intervention. Draw them to you. Make them want to buy, work with you. Develop your digital assets and make them work for you.

Any methodology, patented or not, that you have created is an asset. Expose it. Tell it to the world, to the more people the better. Do not fear that they will copy you, if they do the better (collaboration, and not competition), since they will be amplifying your voice. Your value is not the methodology itself but the way in which you put it into practice as its creator.

Your experience is an asset. Your Personal Brand is an asset. Your self-confidence is an asset. Your creativity is an asset. And of course, the time you dedicate to developing that creativity (reading, training, experimenting, reflecting or carrying out projects on topics that interest you), is not a cost factor, but an investment in your greatest and main asset: your intelligence, the engine of your creativity. I once read a definition of the term *read* that captivated me: "reading is instantly downloading the intelligence of others to your mind." I cannot think of a more genuine way to grow your greatest asset, your intelligence, than to incorporate the assets, the intelligence, of others.

Exercising your intelligence is expanding your comfort zone. It is generating in the mind new concepts, ideas, thoughts and theories and, most importantly, the ability for the mind to connect them together to create new concepts, ideas, thoughts and theories that can help you to give original solutions to problems in that subject that you are passionate about (I'm sure this definition sounds familiar to you: again, creativity). That connection that occurs in the brain, at the neurophysiological level, is called learning. That is right, creativity is learning.

Investing in learning is investing in the ability to create assets. As we said, the exit of *The Rat Race* towards a more authentic existence has a lot to do with creativity, with learning. Creating is learning and learning is creating. Investing in this loop makes a lot more sense than investing in the earn-and-spend loop. But, in addition, when you invest in assets that have to do with what you are passionate about, that time invested multiplies, because it generates new lines of possibilities, actions and connections or synergies with people who are driven by the same causes, which are in congruence with your very essence and that will be new assets that work for your same cause. Do you remember how Artificial Intelligence worked? Opening trees of possibilities to maximize its learning and therefore its probability of success. Why do we limit our natural human ability to be explorers, to lose ourselves for finding new possibilities and connecting our lives to those of others who are naturally driven by the same causes? It makes sense, even financially!

For me it is essential that the exercise that this chapter raises from the financial point of view only applies to what you are passionate about. Therefore, to think at the economic level, we must have made the journey of self-knowledge of purpose and passions and liberation of our creativity previously. Investing in assets related to a certain issue that is no skin off our nose can end up resulting in a passive income. But I have not written this book for people whose objective is to generate income in *auto* mode and go to an island to do nothing, but for people who want to live out of their passions and live leading the way guided by their purpose every day, to leave a trace and a positive legacy in a world that cries out for fewer "leaders" extracting value from its *islands* and more LEADERS helping to ensure that these *islands* are not flooded with our ambition as a species.

Let us break that loop of unconscious production and consumption and help create another loop, a virtuous circle between assets and income, between our intelligence and our actions, between what we learn and what we do, between our consciousness and our creativity. And in the midst of all this, our passions brought to the essence zone, an authentic existence.

The day has 24 hours for everyone. The way in which we dedicate our time from day to day depends on each one of us. If you have your income lines and your balance of assets in mind, you will know at which level you are working with what you do every day. *Working for yourself* does not mean being freelance or setting up a *startup*. It means that what you work on every day has a meaning for you, adds up to your life purpose and boosts your passions, on which you grow in learning and action. Somehow, your time multiplies, because you find the WHATs that work for all of that at the same time. In financial terms, you do not go to work every day to earn a salary that can pay the bills. This is the greatest mental derangement that exists, an inauthentic life. On the other hand, when you *work for yourself,* what you dedicate time to every day boosts your passions, cultivates your assets, and specifically your greatest asset, which is your intelligence. You have fun. You create. You learn. Money comes later and is a consequence of what you do and what you are passionate about. Confucius said, "Find a job that you like and you will not have to work a day of your life." Some call it financial freedom.

There are people who change jobs for a better salary, or when they have promoted a colleague instead of themselves, or when the passing of the years has generated a satiety that weighs too much. There are other people who change jobs when in the current job they have stopped learning. Some, dominated by ego and fears, work for money. Others, from their purpose, work for themselves, make money (their time dedicated to day-to-day work) work for them, to cultivate their assets, to enjoy and expand their passions, to grow their intelligence and promote their creativity, so they can lead their life towards a meaningful purpose.

We live in times of constant change. The ability to learn continuously and the ability to adapt are no longer just desirable skills on a curriculum, but essential survival mechanisms for people. Think about what the term Artificial Intelligence or *Machine Learning* means. Literally, computers that think and learn. The probability that a machine thinks and learns faster than a human is infinite. What a machine cannot compete with is with human passions, the emotion that a passion generates, with the empathy to communicate that passion and bring out emotions, and with the creative capacity of the mind when it connects ideas and people to expand the area of comfort (for example, to create new businesses or jobs that did not exist before). This is what many call Entrepreneurial Attitude and it has already become one of the *soft skills* (or human skills) most in demand in the work environment.

Moreover, I believe that entrepreneurs will define and lead the future of work, regardless of whether we are talking about self-employment or employment, large or small companies established or newly created businesses. I therefore believe that entrepreneurs, who are brave to live on what they are passionate about, be owners of their time, contribute to collective, transcendental and meaningful causes and maintain their independence and authenticity, will lead from their consciousness and from their creativity. And I believe that it will be the creative conscious leaders who will set the rules of business in the era of Artificial Intelligence, because of their ability and willingness to create as well as their ability and willingness to learn, continuously.

Be the example of the creative conscious leader you want to see in business and in the world. Live from what you are passionate about, own your time, contribute to a collective, transcendental and meaningful cause, whose purpose thrills you from within, and keep your independence and authenticity. Lead others from your own example. Be an entrepreneur. That does not mean being self-employed or founding a startup. These are only labor, tax or legal formalities. Being an entrepreneur is an adventurous mindset that I think we all actually have. Well, we are entrepreneurs of our own life project and, with it, of the example with which we lead towards others. Let us all receive it with the gratitude it deserves, assume it with the responsibility it deserves, and live it with the joy it means.

In the industrial age, human beings worked for productivity and efficiency.

In the information age, human beings worked for communication, information and knowledge.

In the age of Artificial Intelligence, the human being will work for the human being. Let us be clear that working for oneself is not a beautiful utopia, but a mechanism of congruence, survival and human leadership in the times we live in. Do yourself a favor and do not use others as an excuse for not doing it yourself, what's more, do it for them, by the example you give them, the education you offer them and the legacy you leave them: work for yourself.

Part IV.

Lead through chaos from your purpose.

After having found happiness and enlightenment in the other world, the hero finds the meaning of return in preserving the wisdom acquired in the search, incorporating that wisdom into a human life, and then finding a way to share it with the rest of the world. The hero manages to find a balance between the material and the spiritual, manages to feel full and competent in both worlds, the everyday and the exceptional, the exterior and the interior.

As we have seen, expanding the comfort zone implies leaving everyday reality to search, discover and learn, but also to return to that reality that has not changed, nor does it want to change, to activate our learnings and transform that reality. A reality that, let us remember:

It is just as volatile, uncertain, complex and ambiguous.

It continues to be in constant evolution and revolution.

It continues to call us to the search for security and stability that do not exist anymore.

It demands more things from us, with higher quality and in less time.

It is led by people whose leadership paradigm is in many cases obsolete, starting with their inability to lead from a meaningful purpose that responds to the real challenges we face as a species today.

It continues forcing us to choose, to specialize and to discard options without hardly knowing them.

After the journey of search, discovery and learning, this part of the journey proposes you the key elements so that the return to your reality is effectively transformative:

KPIs of your life: how to establish an actionable transformative plan and follow it up objectively to ensure that you are walking the path guided by your purpose on a day-to-day basis.

The experience of your entire environment: how to focus on the value you are capable of creating for people as the essence of an authentic life and business model.

The world needs more Intrapreneurs (the true ones): how to be "a peacock in the land of penguins", that is, how to run your authentic life (and business) model, leading from the awareness of your purpose in a challenging and generally adverse environment.

Authenticity is the currency in the trust economy: how to create the foundations to capitalize on the value that you are able to deliver to people.

The leaders of the 21st century: How to bet on a balanced conscious and creative leadership, generous and sustainable in the long term.

Chapter 20

KPIs of your life.

How to establish an actionable transformative plan and follow it up objectively to ensure that you are walking the path guided by your purpose on a day-to-day basis.

The connection with our purpose illuminated the first great discovery of our journey back to reality: creativity. Let us remember its meaning. Creativity is the ability to generate new ideas or concepts that produce original value solutions to real problems. In other words, it is the ability to discover new possibilities and realize them to transform reality.

So far, the journey has invited you to the discovery of possibilities, starting with what connects with your passions, emotions and the design and exploration of your own adventure (the word *entrepreneur* is closely related to the word *adventure*), starting with a momentous finding: the purpose with which to guide the way you lead your own life.

In this part of the journey, we are going to start the part of realization of those possibilities. Possibility is a potential state of reality, one option among many others that, through the execution of a job, becomes realized. We call the planning and execution of this work a *project,* because we project (which comes from the Latin *pro-iectare,* "launch forward"), we imagine how we want reality to be in the future and we identify the steps that need to be taken between the present moment and that future so that this transformation of reality occurs.

In projects, we define the objectives, phases, tasks, owners, milestones, dependencies, needs, associated costs and key metrics. These parameters will help us evaluate whether our transformation project has been successful or not. For this evaluation, we use metrics or indicators.

KPIs (*Key Performance Indicators*) are those key metrics we define in any project to monitor and evaluate if it is on the right track, according to the vision of transformation of the original reality defined by that project.

We have been working with KPIs (also known as OKRs -*Objectives and Key Results*-) for years and companies have deeply rooted them as a mechanism for measuring objectives (which for workers translates, in the best of cases, into payment of an annual bonus). For the KPIs to be complete, a technique called SMART is used, which defines the KPIs as:

S	*Specific*
M	*Measurable*
A	*Attainable*
R	*Relevant*
T	*Timely*

For a KPI to have meaning for a certain project, it must be specific, measurable, achievable, relevant and timely to the project. Makes sense.

The problem of our reality lies in how the structure of KPIs in a company is based on a vision (which, by definition, is not SMART), and cascades down through all the teams and people of the company in the form of SMART KPIs. And, above all, how we evaluate whether or not the fulfillment of those KPIs keeps the company in the right direction guided by its vision or not. I think that, in this translation of the vision to the plan, from the abstract to the concrete, many emotional, human nuances are lost (which represents the vision or the purpose of any project) and we end up lost in the measurement of the specific, the quantitative, the timings, the numbers.

I am not saying it is simple. It is not, far from it. What I do know is that great leaders have a clear vision, a firm purpose, and are capable of articulating concrete objectives that materialize the day-to-day journey, the steps guided by that purpose, without falling into the disorientation of numbers and short-term goals. They draw a medium-long-term plan and are consistent in short-term actions to move forward in the right direction.

Let's look at this through a case. I have recently taught Creative Thinking and Entrepreneurial Attitude classes, within a *soft skills* learning program, whose purpose was to train the leaders of the 21st century in fundamental human skills so that they would be able to transform and lead the era of Artificial Intelligence. About 30 people went through the program. If you had to choose one metric to measure the success or non-success of the program, what would it be? I give you some ideas:

Total income per each edition.

Number of students per each edition.

Number of editions made per year.

Total income per year.

Number of cities in which we have implemented the program.

Acquisition cost per each student.

Net profit.

Percentage of students who have recommended the program to other people, who have been new students.

Percentage of students who, at the end of the program, declare that they have been transformed personally and professionally.

If I had to choose only one of these KPIs (what is known as OMTM - *one metric to measure*, the key metric to measure), I would, without a doubt, choose the percentage of students who declare themselves transformed after completing the program. Let us think about it: what do the rest of the metrics inform us about? Revenues, number of students per edition, number of cities activated or net profit are metrics that tell us nothing about the essence of the program, what connects with the vision or purpose for which it was created: its ability to revive human skills in people and transform them into leaders of the 21st century.

As I pointed out before, the problem is that these metrics are generally not very objective: how do we quantify what it is like to have been transformed or not? That is the challenge. Meaningful metrics are not easily quantifiable, although they are tangible. A person perceives, feels, senses when another has been transformed. That perception, sensitivity, intuition are human abilities that play a fundamental role in the way we lead but that, for some reason, have been seriously reviled in the traditional executive world, embodied in what we have called the leader of the 20th century.

The leader of the 20th century is a leader driven by short-term goals. The bonus. The promotion. Competitiveness with teammates. The possibility of losing his position to the rumored layoffs. Egos and fears. And that makes the vision of the company, the purpose for which that company exists, vanish in its structure. And the structure itself falls prey to financial metrics that do not report at all about the value that company is delivering to its customers, the original purpose for which it was created.

Taken on a personal level, I think it is very relevant to ask what we should measure day by day to ensure that we are executing our transformation project, guided by its vision or purpose. Define the KPIs of our life. And try to make them as SMART as possible. Without allowing our purpose to fade into numbers and short-term objectives or needs, but without leaving it to chance or the constant future, and acting to walk the path we want to walk. Make a plan that it is guided by purpose and principles.

Look at the metrics that you are indeed measuring day by day. Use critical thinking and reflect about how many times a week you take actions like these:

Unlock the mobile phone to see if you have any WhatsApp.

Check how many *likes* your last post on Instagram has had.

Check how many followers you have on Twitter.

Access Facebook to "see what's new."

What do these everyday actions bring us? What metric do they respond to? What goal do they build? What project do they belong to? By what ultimate purpose are they guided? Eric Ries, author of the book *"Lean Startup"*, defines these metrics as *Vanity Metrics*, which give us a lot of instant comfort, in the sense that they feed our ego (if followed, appreciated, recognized) or even reduce our fear (of missing out, for example), but they are not actionable, in the sense that they do not allow us to support a project, a plan with a meaning, with a vision, with a purpose.

Not only that, but while we are performing all these small actions repeatedly day by day, we are absent from the reality that we have around us, we stop being present in it and we abandon that state of mindful consciousness that we convened is so necessary in this hyper-connected world.

We do not realize it, but, as in the case of the leaders of the 20th century, if these actions take over our everyday life and generate artificial needs, we can end up dedicating an important part of our most valuable resources (time, attention and yes, money as well) and eventually our life project becomes a slave to those artificial needs, devoid of any purpose.

Let us turn this around. Start from the vision, from your purpose. Those reflections that you made after the discovery in chapter 14 are what will help you establish your plan, your project, your objectives and the metrics or KPIs that support its execution. For example, if my purpose is to help people release their creative essence so that they can lead their projects in a more authentic way to make the world a more human place, it makes sense that I set more concrete goals that help me walk this path that guides my purpose:

Help others to approach their goals from a prism more connected to who they are.

Do executive counselling from the focus of consciousness and creativity.

Facilitate workshops, talks, courses and projects related to the education of human skills in the digital age.

Be a good parent, partner, and friend.

And, going even more to the concrete, to measure whether I am taking the correct steps in the direction towards the achievement of those objectives day by day, it makes sense that I ask myself questions like:

How many people have I listened to and helped this week?

How many smiles of people who did not have a good day have I raised today?

How many people have I inspired with my mindful creative leadership proposals this month?

How much time have I spent writing (articles, a book) on mindful creative leadership this week?

How many projects related to human skills education have I carried out this year?

How much quality time have I spent with my children today?

How much quality time have I spent with my partner today?

How much quality time have I spent with my friends this week?

Those are the KPIs of my life. When I say that these KPIs, the objectives they pursue and the purpose they support, should not fade into short-term needs, I mean that it is easy to fall into the "I had a bad day today, so I'll do the helping others thing tomorrow", or the "today I've had a lot of trouble at work, which is what feeds me, so I'll deal with the education projects when I have time."

Working for yourself means that your day-to-day life and your journey guided by your purpose are exactly the same thing. That the *trouble* of any day at work helps me to help other people, builds my purpose, is my life plan. Creativity and Entrepreneurial Attitude are, in fact, closely linked. In other words, my day-to-day creation needs and, therefore, my actions, what I put focus, attention, time and financial resources on, are exactly the actions that my assets generate, that build my unique and authentic adventure, my own vital company, the path guided by my purpose.

If the succession of *bad days* or *with a lot of trouble* make up our day to day, it is time to stop and think to get back on track, because clearly the vision of *your vital company* has vanished and the plan is not being followed (we are like the captain who wanted to make it to Cabo de Palos but who sails on *autopilot* drinking a Gin Tonic and never reaches the destination he set in the first place). In the same way, the cost item of your personal income statement should not be a disaster drawer of expense entries that you do not know very well what need they respond to, what objective they pursue, what plan they support and what purpose they contribute to. While most people spend as much as their income allows them to live “the best possible life”, conscious leaders design their cost structure to support exactly the needs they have identified to meet the KPIs in their plan that contribute to their personal purpose. This minimalism, essentialism or conscious consumption (whatever we want to call it) is a really liberating mindset so that your vital company can really be led by your purpose.

Reconnect with your purpose. Write it down on a sheet of paper. Stick it on the wall of your office, look at it every day, do not lose sight of it. Define what are the objectives that support that purpose and define the KPIs of your life, those small steps that will tell you if you are meeting your objectives, walking the path guided by your purpose and therefore living, the life you want to live. Write them down, invest in the needs (time, costs) that you have to meet them and measure them day by day. Modify the list frequently, as you expand your comfort zone, learning, growing your assets, connecting each time in a more intimate way what you would like to do in your life and what you actually do day by day. Do not stop measuring those KPIs of your life. Get up every day satisfied with what you did yesterday and keen on what you are going to do today. Look at your purpose on the wall and smile back.

Have you observed how great leaders inspire in a balanced, calm and consistent way even though their environment is just as rapid and changing as anyone else's? Their purpose and the consistency of their actions with that purpose are the reasons for this strength.

The environment is changing and chaotic. But you have started to lead in it from your purpose. And external changes that were once a threat are now opportunities to learn, create and reinforce the path you lead.

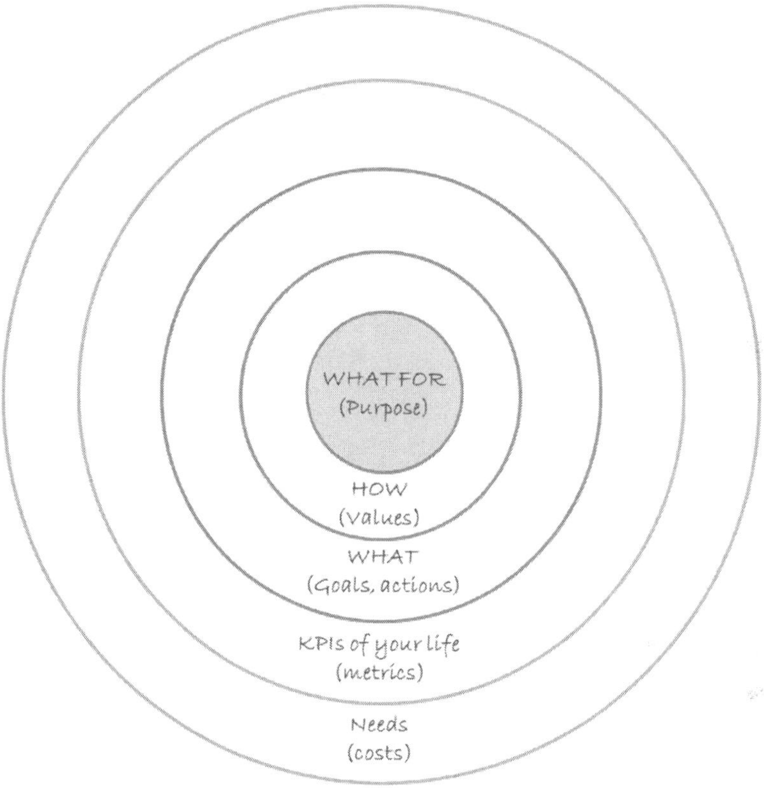

The Golden Circle, by Simon Sinek, extended.

The KPIs of your life are the metrics with which you will measure how the path guided by your purpose materializes. Now the challenge is how to make your purpose bring value, through the experience of the people around you, so that it can be also be transformed into a business model.

Chapter 21

The experience of your entire enviroment.

How to focus on the value you are capable of creating for people as the essence of an authentic life and business model.

Much has been said in the last years of Experience.

Customer Experience appeared as a revulsive in the business world, bringing together disciplines such as design, customer research or usability and appearing like a mantra of customer loyalty for which it was necessary to count on the very little cheap service of very smart consultants to help you worry that your customers have a good experience using your products and services.

I do not want to be misunderstood. I am a huge advocate of Customer Experience and the awareness work that these consultants have done and continue to do. For me, Customer Experience is something as basic and human as understanding the fact that people will repeat those experiences of which they have good memories. And, in a world of endless options, this is a treasure for any product, service, business, or brand. What caught my attention in those years of revolution was precisely that, that it meant a revolution:

- "From now on, we are going to design our products focusing on the customer" - "Of course! And who have we focused them on so far though?" - I thought, maybe young and naive.

- "The Customer Experience of a product is not only the use of the product, but the entire customer journey from its discovery and onboarding, going through errors, doubts and complaints that may arise, until its cancellation" - "Yes, of course, that's why we carefully and fondly design the customer experience with our product at all touchpoints throughout the User Journey."

Putting customers at the center and focusing on providing maximum value through their expertise. It seemed so basic that I discovered that something had not been done well for years, maybe decades, in the design of products and services in the business world to make this Customer Experience sound so revolutionary. Perhaps the structured methodologies of divergent thinking with which this discipline was worked on. But the fact that an organization that exists by and for bringing value to its customers (that is, "putting the customer at the center") sounded innovative, revealed many inefficiencies of organizations beyond even their product design departments, in their cultural nucleus, a symptom of their *titulitis aguda*, of the excessive hierarchical burden in their leadership and in their too closed *corporate career* approach to the professional and personal development of their employees. In any case, I was glad that this wave caught me with the wetsuit on, the board and the muscles ready and in the right place to surf it.

Later the discipline transcended to other settings, which was to be expected. The Employee Experience (also called, from the point of view of the employing company, Employer Branding). That is, "what do I do as a company to be attractive and that the best talent wants to work with me and stay?" This is a great and beautiful journey that many companies are still traveling. Because it raises questions that have been silenced for a long time and whose answers can only be found by addressing the company's culture at its roots. Years ago, companies hired only on their name or reputation for job security, or by offering appealing positions and salaries. Today we know that the companies that have stayed there have great difficulties in hiring and *retaining* talent. Thinking about the experience of its employees or, what is the same, in its *Employer Branding*, has opened the mind of many companies and has predisposed them to a deep internal change to reconnect with their essence, their mission, vision and values, and get all dressed up to attract and retain talent. Another great joy that I took with me.

If we take these reflections to the personal level, we have to address the field of Personal Branding. I am interested in the territory of the Personal Brand because it is something that sounds familiar to everyone -in some way, it attracts them- and to which at the same time I saw a brutal improvement journey, mainly due to the incomplete use that has been made of the term over the years, as if your goal was somehow to sell yourself. Selling yourself to get a better position, a promotion, change jobs... in short, sell yourself for money.

I realized that this was the real reason why the emergence of the CX (Customer eXperience) and later the EX (Employee eXperience) were so powerful and revolutionary. Again the money. Companies had spent decades with financial targets as the ultimate reason of their existence. And of course, in this context, what is more important: to audit and improve the processes for handling customer complaints for the entire portfolio of current products and services, or to focus team resources and money on launching new products that will generate new lines of short-term income? And what is more critical: to analyze and improve the root causes why your employees give you a 6 out of 10 in the employee satisfaction index, or to launch cost-cutting initiatives to maximize the margin of the financial year of the ongoing year? There was a lack of authentic purpose, which would bring the person back to the center of the company.

The term Experience (of customers, of employees) really had an impact on companies when they realized that their competition in the digital age offered countless alternatives to those customers and employees and, in many cases, much better. Alternatives usually coming from incoming players who do not have an income statement to protect and who design those experiences by and for customers (and employees) from the very beginning. And, of course, then they keep them.

Experience is something that overgrew financials. It was simply addressing something greater than money: human happiness. The welfare of a customer whose credit cards have been stolen and who in a call (or better, in a few clicks in the bank's app) is able to cancel them and request new ones. Or the realization of an employee who works for a company whose mission is to reduce the amount of plastic in the seas and has creatively devised slippers whose soles are made of this plastic, removed from the sea, this mission being in total harmony with the personal purpose of that employee. And this paradigm break was what gave the territory of Experience that power of irruption into the business world. As I thought when I was way youngster, what underlies these disciplines of customer or employee experience is nothing more than common sense. But the context looked the other way, and their great purpose gave it the entity that they have today.

Returning to the field of Personal Branding, I see that the widespread belief that this is a discipline "to sell oneself better" is the perfect breeding ground for this field (*Personal Branding*) to happen, the same thing that happened years ago with Customer Experience or Employer Branding: that it will go massive.

For me, Personal Branding is much more than how you sell yourself. The purest, simplest and most powerful definition that satisfied me is the following:

Your Personal Brand is what others perceive of you.

Powerful, right? Because who likes others to perceive us negatively? Nobody. We all want to add value to our environment and for our environment to perceive it. In other words, it is a universal need. A meaningful, powerful purpose.

In that definition, I use "others" in the broadest sense of the word. Another mistake regarding the term Personal Brand, in my opinion, has been linking it exclusively to online environments. It seems that only those who have 10k+ followers on social networks have a Personal Brand, those we call influencers or, simply, those who publish the most. Let there be no mistake. The digital revolution has opened the door to the interconnection of people, regardless of their physical location. But even someone disconnected from the online world has a personal brand. The rude baker of my town comes to mind. He has offline Personal Brand (the opinion of his customers who obviously share it with the rest of the town) and of course online (those same opinions published on Google, TripAdvisor, Facebook, Foursquare...). As Enrique Dans, a professor at IE, says, "you exist on the Internet, whether you like it or not."

I also consider a mistake to link the term Personal Brand exclusively to professional environments. I ask myself, "Can you be a good leader without being a good father or mother, partner or person?" I don't think so. Moreover, I do not believe that there is a personal self and a professional self. I understand the reasons why we have historically wanted to separate both *worlds*, but I also believe that, in the current context, this is no longer useful and not actually possible. Today the world is more liquid than ever, we change jobs between 10 and 14 times throughout our professional lives, we will work with friends, our coworkers will become part of our personal environment, we will need to relate professionally with people of our personal environment. In the age of Artificial Intelligence, people need to engage people, and unlock that personal sensitivity, empathy, and vulnerability that have long been synonymous with executive weakness. Having two faces (one professional and the other personal, one facing the collaborators and the other facing the personal environment, family and friends) does not help that consistency and authenticity that today has turned, as obvious as it may seem, into a basic value of every leader.

Another mistake is linking the Personal Brand concept exclusively to the near physical or temporary environment. It is no longer worth seeking the benefit of the near environment if this has a negative impact on the other side of the world, or sacrifices the medium-long term. The current context demands sustainable leaders, who look and care about the repercussion of their actions in the medium-long term and in the whole environment, in society, on the planet. Society begins to have an awareness of our individual and collective responsibility for the sustainability of the planet, and we begin to speak of GPI companies or companies that Generate a Positive Impact on society and on the planet. The leaders of these companies are not satisfied with financial objectives and understand the growth of their company and their personal brand, linked to generating a positive impact on the environment, working to leave a positive legacy in the world, and growing with it.

Each and every one of us (whether we like it or not) has a personal brand, which is what others (be it a friend, a customer, someone who finds you on the Internet, a supplier you have in India or, ultimately, anyone who lives together in the same environment as you, the World) think of us. And, since you have a personal brand, why not work on it so that it is an asset that in turn works for you, that helps you live the life you want to live, that adds up to your purpose?

The good news is that personal brand is worked on. It should be worked on, in my opinion. And this is another aspect that makes this field interesting: the speed with which one can see results. Because we are all human (for now), and we have the ability to observe, feel, empathize, forgive, love. A detail, a change of attitude, an apology, build your personal brand in the minds of others and this reinforces your authentic leadership, from the purpose. I invite you to do something, right now, as you read these lines:

Grab your phone, open your text messaging app, scroll down, scroll down, scroll down, keep scrolling down, scroll down further... stop! Open the chat you had with that contact (contact, not group). Write exactly: "How are you?" Hit send.

Do not change the sentence. Do not change your contact. It does not matter if it is an ex, the doorman of your mom's house, the CEO of your company or the maid you had last year. Send him or her a "how are you?" and wait to for the answer.

I have done this little dynamic with hundreds of people, executives or not. As trivial as it may seem, the results are impressive. From receiving a nice "Great, thank you very much! And you, how are you?" in response, to provoking a coffee with someone they had not seen for too long. And in most cases, a change of attitude of the person who sent that "trivial" text, who discovered how powerful it is to be attentive, to be thoughtful. It is striking, but sometimes we do not realize how this hyper-connectivity demand for immediacy of the context makes "the every day life eats us up" without paying attention to the details, and after a while we realize that we have been for years without seeing a relative, without offering our help to a friend or without really being interested in how our partner is doing. How can we expect to add authentic value to those who, from our professional *self,* we call customers, if we cannot even be thoughtful with our nearest personal environment?

And it is that, if you have been able to have a gesture with the maid that you had a year ago or with that friend that you had not seen for a while, have it with your partner, closest friends, coworkers and people that you have closer day by day, it is much easier. And the feeling is incredibly rewarding. The power of the little things.

I invite you to do more little things:

Go on a Saturday morning to see that relative you have not seen for a long time.

Approach a coworker tomorrow and ask, "Can I give you a hand with something?"

Call that person with whom you have a dispute and tell him that you want to buy him a beer to fix it.

Post on your Facebook wall: "Hello! Does anyone need me for something today?"

Prepare a tasty breakfast for your partner.

Acknowledge someone's work publicly on your Linkedin.

Play a whole evening with your children without grabbing your phone at all.

Ask your boss how she is doing.

Ask the waiter who serves you coffee every day how the week is going.

Thank your mother.

Send a "How are you?" text to someone on every day.

Take interest in others, their aspirations and their frustrations. More network is built in 2 months by taking interest in others than in 2 years trying to get others to be interested in you. Do not look for the reasons why you cannot do all of this. They are just excuses. It is your Personal Brand: the way others perceive your leadership style. Excuses are traps you set for yourself. Change the speech. Be the owner of your time and your actions. Cultivate that great asset which is the value that others perceive in you.

If you develop a routine of help, suddenly the *trivialities* of the day to day become minor problems, reasons to be better, small satisfactions, and cause changes in others. Attention to details, day by day. That is your Personal Brand. The experience of others. The experience of your entire environment.

Customer Experience is the reason why customers will buy a certain product or brand in the end. The value of that brand. Employee Experience is the reason why employees will eventually choose to join or stay to work at a certain company. The value of that company. The Experience of your entire environment is the reason why in the end those who interact with you will recognize you as an authentic and proposeful leader, whatever you do. Your value.

And, like Customer Experience and Employee Experience, the Experience of your whole environment (your Personal Brand) is not born by and for selling more. It is born due to the essential purpose of offering better experiences to those who are going to enjoy those experiences, whatever it is that you have to offer. It is not about selling more. It is about having a meaningful purpose, about designing a plan to implement a transformative project guided by that purpose and about leading your life consequently to that project. It is about being yourself day by day, doing what you are passionate about and doing well, doing it with care and attention to detail, adding value to others and being recognized for it. Money will be a consequence of that, if so decided by the designer of a certain experience and, of course, if the person who enjoys it perceives that value.

In the world of immediacy and lack of time in which we live, attention to detail is a differential factor. I invite you to think about what specific details you can have day by day to improve the experience of your whole environment, add value to others and fulfill the KPIs of your life that materialize your purpose. This is not only the best way of self-realization, but the principle of transformation of the reality that surrounds you, through others, through collaboration with others, making your network a real asset and earning you the recognition of others to build your Personal Brand, your authentic and proposeful leadership. The one through which you can work for yourself, in congruence between what you want to be and what you are day by day, wherever you work. In the next chapter, we will see how to do it, even when you work for a large company.

Chapter 22

The world needs more Intrapreneurs (the true ones).

How to be "a peacock in the land of penguins", that is, how to run your authentic life (and business) model, leading from the awareness of your purpose in a challenging and generally adverse environment.

A time has come when large corporations have realized that they need to change course if they want to innovate and bet on future growth. Of course, the growth of their business, but also, and closely linked to it, the talent they handle and their ability to attract, develop and *retain*.

The startup culture attracts and develops people's talent by focusing on people (not on the company's "human resources"), their real aspirations and frustrations as humans, seeking the feeling of belonging through common purpose, where people are proudly driven by the company to which they belong (as opposed to the culture of "leave your emotions and personal matters at the entrance of this office, here you come to work"), with a transparent and open approach (against the information underground economy), a horizontal management model (compared to the prevalence of hierarchy), in which diversity is encouraged and in which safe environments are created for exploration, wanting errors to occur quickly and cheaply to maximize learning (in opposition to the widespread acceptance that failure is falling down and therefore better not trying).

Attracting this entrepreneurial talent to the traditional corporate structure is a practically impossible task. People look for a culture in which all of the above naturally belongs to the DNA of the company, and the purpose and values of the company are shared by all team members. This talent is no longer motivated by a salary or an attractive position if the environment in which it is going to have to develop is unnatural and incongruous for them.

The Entrepreneurial Attitude is a mental state of consciousness of people who have understood their purpose and values and seek or create projects congruent with them.

The first time I defined Entrepreneurial Attitude in this way was in an Intrapreneurship workshop for a multinational company in the insurance sector. And I added: "to me this state feels very similar to happiness."

There are those who define an entrepreneur as the person who works on his own. There are those who define an entrepreneur as the person who works in a startup. For me, being entrepreneurship is an attitude, and it is independent of being self-employed or employed, or working for a startup or a large corporation. It has to do with an adventurous spirit of exploration and transformation, which is transversal to the legal model of the relationship between person and company or its size. What is true is that working on your own helps you connect your vision with what you do every day. Just as working in a smaller company helps you to identify you with the vision and values of the company in a closer way, as well as to ensure that what that company does every day is congruent with that vision and those values that you share.

Working for yourself is not working on your own or in a startup, but rather finding that congruence with your vision and values regardless of the place or company where you work. Most of the people, in fact, today work for others. And many work in medium or large companies. That is why I am interested in addressing this specific case, that of the employed person in a medium or large company, and analyze it in detail to look for the alternatives that the conscious and creative leader has to find its consistency in the day by day without having to, necessarily, break with it radically. If working as an employee in medium or large companies is not a case that affects or interests you and you prefer, at this point, to skip the analysis that I detail below, you can take your entrepreneurial attitude directly to the next chapter. When in doubt, I invite you to enter into the analysis that, although detailed and applied to the case of large companies, I believe that it can provide you with learning for any work environment (in the end, it is about creating value through the experience of your customer and your whole environment, as we said in the previous chapter).

I have personally worked for years as an employee, costumer, supplier and partner for large corporations and what I have observed over the course of time is that the traditional mechanisms of their culture end up causing in many of their employees a strong disconnection between their work and how they behave in their personal life. As we saw previously, I do not believe that there are two lives, professional and personal. So this seems to me, simply, living incongruously.

Aware that the new talent no longer accepts this, corporations have adopted several strategies over time to try to reverse this situation and try to remain competitive in the talent race in which we are immersed in the 21st century.

Work with design and strategic innovation consultancies.

Generally, these companies work with a startup culture, transparent, open to error to maximize learning, collaborative, creative, innovative, focused on the customer experience. At the same time, they know and strongly empathize with the corporate cultures that hire them, either from experience, specialization or because some of the members of their team worked within them.

Their work methodologies are disruptive, totally different from what an ordinary day can be in a large company. They are based on observation and field exploration ("leave the office and go where your customers are to listen to them carefully and in depth"), on the design mindset ("don't focus on your product and your company, focus on solving the problems of your customers and on making their experience excellent"), in agile processes (construction of minimal prototypes to cause errors quickly and cheaply and maximize learning throughout the process) and in visual collaboration (covering the walls with murals and post-its is not just something trendy and fancy; there is evidence that the brain creates more associations, goes deeper into concepts when it visualizes information, which also favors collaboration between team members since it causes externalisation of ideas, incubation and debate).

It is true that this is probably the best way to create a revulsive in a work team of a traditional company. However, it is essential to create the right context internally, from the direction of that company. A safe environment to establish a favorable context for this revulsive. Otherwise, the external input of the work with the consultancy will not be credible or will be taken with extreme caution by the team members, aware that in the culture in which they live day by day, these innovative techniques represent a disruption. And for anyone it is safer to stay in the rear and wait to see if a disruption stalls or not, than to risk sticking their heads out to spearhead that transformation. Having an open mind is a fundamental premise for the work of innovation consultancies to be effective. However, an open mind is part of that long-awaited Entrepreneurial Attitude, and therefore part of the solution, which presents the first dilemma of this model.

The second dilemma, critical to me, is that the work of external consultants is, by definition, temporary (let's ignore the indefinite consulting projects in which in the end the consultant is just another employee of the corporation, with the difference that his salary is paid by someone else; here there is neither methodological revulsive nor cultural disruption, but a mere fiscal or labor convenience for some companies that does not deserve more than a couple of lines).

Innovation consultancies execute a temporary project for their corporate customers. During a defined time (typically between 3 and 6 months), customer teams leave their comfort zone, work differently on a real problem of their company, acquire techniques of customer discovery, creative thinking, collaboration, agile project management and service design, shape new projects and generally have a lot of fun.

But what happens next? How does the management of the company (the one that created an atmosphere of mental openness at the beginning of the project) makes sure that the return of this team to the reality of the day by day is safe and transformative? In the end, what you have is a team that has gone through something different, revulsive, for a while and that now returns to the day-to-day context, which has not changed and will put all the antibodies to work to prevent the different element sinks in the system. In other words, how does the company ensure that its entire structure expands its comfort zone with the learning achieved from the expedition that came out of it?

As interesting as answering these questions may seem, my experience from both sides -corporate customers and consultancies- is devastating. Just as much as the speed at which this new way of working inoculated by the consultancy vanishes when it is mixed again with the dominant corporate culture. The only things left are small mindset changes in some people, but who do not feel comfortable executing them within the corporate culture. There begins the incongruity we spoke about before.

The reality is that any path of transformation runs on a daily basis. Not for 3 or 6 months, but continuously, in the day-to-day business. The design and innovation mindset must be within the company, in project meetings, in the Steering Committees. I think that a temporary revulsive is very good (sometimes essential), but I also think that it is not enough.

Create realities parallel to the corporate culture itself.

Many large companies around the world have created new divisions to address this future sustainable growth and the problem of attracting and developing talent. Telefónica, Santander, BBVA, even traditional business consultancies such as Accenture, Indra or Everis are some examples of large Spanish companies that have invested in forming their own divisions, which they named *digital* (due to the association of the elements of this Entrepreneurial Attitude with digital reality, open, agile, changing).

The goal is to equip this new division with assets so that it has the ability to start from scratch. That is, mixing the best of the startup world (attitude, culture, philosophy) with the best of the corporate world (access to markets, customers, data, brand recognition, budget). In theory, it is a good recipe.

The first thing these companies should avoid is the temptation to *fill in* these new divisions with employees from the culture that is intended to evolve. It is something radical and we should not generalize, but I think that, during the first years, the objective for which a new division is created must be taken care of to the maximum possible extent: a new culture to attract new talent and new business. That implies starting with a Managing Director with that mindset, with vision and ability to create culture and team, and with autonomy to decide what is good or not for that new unit under these principles, even though some of the proposals come from the president in the matrix.

The second challenge is to design very carefully the way in which this new division is going to rely on the assets of the parent company to operate. Those assets (access to the market, customers, data, etc.), will be *guarded* by the operating business units, say, of the traditional culture. At the beginning of this chapter, we mentioned the information underground economy. We must accept that, for a long time in closed environments such as large companies, information has been power (to a large extent, it continues to be so internally today). And that has caused a certain information underground economy, a kind of invisible accounting fed by a bubble of internal *debits and credits* that forge power relations. I believe that the fact that externally technological evolution has radically democratized access to information is causing that bubble to deflate. In any case, the bubble exists. And the way in which the assets of the traditional culture are made available to the new *digital* culture in the company is something that should not be left to chance, since the mechanisms of traditional culture have all the bargaining power, and then we return to the square one on that path of cultural transformation that we undertook.

I think they are two highly complex challenges to handle in a traditional corporate culture. And, as in the cycle of consciousness of any person, I believe that the traditional corporate culture itself must overcome the phase of mastering its egos and its fears. Which is not easy, much less instantaneous, but a process that can take years and in which many forces come into play.

In this process, let us remember, we are trying to attract and develop new talent to ensure the survival of the business in a new context. A talent called *digital* for its mentality of flexibility and adaptation to continuous change through a philosophy of trial - error - learning. Talent with an Entrepreneurial Attitude. Taking care of these basic aspects, the culture of the new division of the company has, by all means, a lot of appeal. At the base, a purpose of transformation of a *modus operandi* that must evolve because it does not work in a radically different context. On this, values aligned with an entrepreneurial and digital attitude. And on this, additionally, the ability to offer good positions and salaries. Hard not to be attracted. Additionally, in the process of attraction and onboarding, that talent is not treated as a mere candidate, but is really told why the company is looking for people like him or her, people with the ability to lead the company in the change, tell them where to go and what to do, people capable of bringing innovation to the company, being a key part of the transformation project, helping the company to transform, while they themselves develop as professionally and personally.

It is a very beautiful story in theory. And I think it is more powerful in terms of transformation than the case of consultancy firms. But again, my experience tells me that there is something missing. I have observed the path of entrepreneurial talent joining the big company and, unfortunately, in many cases it ends in frustration, even in the case of appealing talent programs in the most innovative divisions of the company.

There is a fable that illustrates this wonderful journey: "A Peacock in the Land of Penguins" (Barbara 'BJ' Hateley, Warren H. Schmidt). I will summarize it for you in my own words.

It tells that in the land of the penguins there was a day when they realized that they had to do different things if they wanted to survive and they went on an inspirational journey to the island of exotic birds. In it, they observed eagles gliding, ostriches running fast through the field and peacocks displaying their colorful and creative beauty. They decided they needed to incorporate some of that talent into the land of the penguins so that they too could learn those arts, be lighter, faster, more creative. To be transformed, in short, to survive. They raised the project to a peacock, that accepted without hesitation. In the land of the penguins, the peacock worked hard to show his natural gifts to the penguins and help them in their transformation project: he ran, displayed his colorful plumage, made short flights and emitted attractive squawks. Before long, he noticed that something was wrong. The penguins watched him with suspicion. After all, they were penguins, they didn't know how to do all those wonderful things, and they were envious of the peacock. He consulted with one of the penguins and he recommended him to reduce the intensity of his movements a little, to run more slowly, not to fly. So that he would look more like the penguins and in this way not to arouse so much jealousy. The peacock tried. But it didn't work. In the end, all the penguins looked at their long and colorful tail and remembered that they could never show it off it like him: they were penguins. Another realiable penguin for the peacock then recommended him to cover his back with a suit. A penguin suit. So that he would be more like them and not cause so much mistrust. The peacock agreed. And he agreed to other similar advice that followed. Little by little the peacock began to stop behaving like a peacock and to be sad. He was not accepted and he did not feel himself. He wondered why he was there. And he recalled the project that they had entrusted to him: "we penguins need other birds to teach us different skills." However, the opposite had happened: he had turned into a penguin. Frustrated, he took off his penguin jacket and with a great squawk unfolded his colorful feathers to return to the island of exotic birds.

The moral, as you imagine, is that any system will react naturally against disruptions that involve a change in the system, since it will identify them as a threat, despite the fact that it was the system itself that detected the need for these disruptions and that change.

This is the story of many of those *digital* talents or those with an *entrepreneurial attitude* who are attracted by the transformation projects of large companies, but who soon realize that their *arts* are not being recognized, valued, sometimes not even used. Traditional culture has then throttled the transformative project and they, after one or two years of trying, find themselves in a limbo from which there are usually only two ways out: accepting that the penguin suit does not look that bad or flying back to the island of exotic birds.

Obviously, the case that interests me is the second, because that spark of Entrepreneurial Attitude is still alive. And, although this entrepreneurial talent is now outside the traditional culture, it has had contact with it and has incorporated into its experience how it is lived in this type of culture, what are its strengths and weaknesses, its opportunities and threats. Somehow, that talent has left its comfort zone and has come back with learnings. Which has a lot of value for that (intra)entrepreneur who follows his path.

However, the traditional culture, the one that wanted to transform, is still in its comfort zone. Which brings us to another dead end.

Well, I think there is another alternative.

Introduce Intrapreneurs (the true ones) in the *core* of the corporate culture.

First, let me explain why the "the true ones" qualification. What large corporations have understood by Intrapreneurship until now was for me a poisonous mixture for everyone, company and employee. The formula was the following: for a certain idea, research or business opportunity (let's call it an innovation project) the company needs a person who dedicates himself for a short period of time (3 to 6 months) to do some research, shape the idea, hypothesize around the idea, explore its potential customers, prototype the idea, validate it with those potential customers, learn, shape a business model canvas and try to find the so-called problem-solution fit. What large corporations have understood as what the company does is to look for a person in the traditional structure of the company and assign him this challenge under certain conditions:

During the investigation period, he keeps his salary that he previously had.

If, after the research period, the hypotheses have been validated and it is considered that the idea and its business model could work for the company, the company takes control of that initiative and, typically, will create a business unit within the correspondent structure in order to finish designing its value proposition, launch it on the market and operate the business. The place that the "intrapreneur" occupies in this new context is uncertain and probably depends more on its capacity for political play than on his (more than likely) good dexterity in leading the initiative that he himself has shaped.

If, on the contrary, after the research period it has not been possible to prove that there is an opportunity for the company in the field in which the idea resided, the "intrapreneur" returns to the unit to which he belonged before and which was saving him the place (and the salary, which never varied). I mean, you take the blue pill and you remember nothing.

Regarding this model, placed in the context where we are discussing the need for more traditional companies to attract and develop digital and entrepreneurial talent, I ask myself: what sort of tenacity in the face of risk are we fostering in a person who maintains his salary regardless of what he does? How are we equating this person's context to that of an entrepreneur's real context: volatile, uncertain, complex, and ambiguous? What is the motivation of this "intrapreneur" if the post-research situation has a high probability of remaining the same as before, regardless of what happens in that research? How do you recognize internally and externally the courage of that person who, somehow, has proactively left his comfort zone? Or a question more essential than all these and it will make you really rack your brains: what real freedom have we given to the "intrapreneur" to validate or refute his hypotheses if all his internal movements during the validation phase have been conditioned by a traditional culture, which is precisely what we want to change?

I have observed some companies whose intrapreneurship model slightly improves on the model noted above. Some offer the "intrapreneur" the possibility of keeping a part of the equity of the new company that will be created as a result of validating the new business model. Others endow the "intrapreneur" with a certain level of autonomy that has been communicated and agreed with the entire traditional structure. However, the story is the same. The previous questions have no answer and that long-awaited search for the Entrepreneurial Attitude in the company does not finish bearing fruit.

In my opinion, the solution is to incorporate Intrapreneurs (the true ones) and give them freedom and responsibilities in the *core* of the business and company culture.

Those Intrapreneurs, "the true ones", are those people whose mentality is aligned with the following basic principles:

They share the purpose and values of the company. They have agreed to enter into a company transformation project whose vision they personally share and that generates a powerful and two-way value bond between the

Intrapreneur and the company that forms the basis of the relationship. The moment something in the traditional company fails at the foundations of that vision execution project, they will continue their way out of the company.

They are conscious, balanced people. The project in which they embark is ecological in their personal balance and together with the company, they establish the foundations so that it continues to be so over time.

They are humble, flexible and empathetic people, capable of experiencing the company's culture from the inside and understanding it firsthand in order to help transform it.

They are creative people, with their own personal brand, and as such they have their own plan and participate in other projects, presentations, workshops, courses and communities outside the company and will continue to do so during the life of the project, since this, among other things, gives a differential value to the contribution of this person with respect to the talent that is already in the company. Their personal brand is not transformed into a position by collaborating with the company as an Intrapreneur. That is to say, it is clear that the company that has incorporated a peacock and the foundations are established so that they do not end up disguising him as a penguin.

They are people with a very high sense of responsibility and committed to achieving the results that will define the project as a success, because it will also be their personal success.

They are free people with critical independence, who must be given autonomy and confidence to execute and demand responsibility based on results.

They are authentic people, who do not need to hide their emotions behind a corporate mask. Their purpose is the reason why they share a project with that company, with that group of people, so they flagship that purpose, communicate it loud and clear and lead from it, provoke emotions, create followers by influence of value regardless of the hierarchical position.

Their leadership is human-centric. People come first, before tasks, processes, short-term needs, and financial goals. Employees, customers, society: people always come first.

These are the key aspects that are part of the Intrapreneurs that the world needs in order for the Entrepreneurial Attitude to take hold in large, more traditional companies. Look now at the aspects that are NOT part of this profile and their relationship with the company:

The legal figure of hiring. That is, if the Intrapreneur collaborates with the company on the payroll, with a part-time contract or as a self-employed *freelancer*. Even at this point, we could extend all the reflections in this chapter to entrepreneurs of their own business. They will also have customers to serve. What difference does it make if they are customers you serve from your company or customers you serve as a consultant or customers you serve as an employee? They are customers. Better said: they are people. Business B2B (Business to Business) or B2C (Business to Consumer): in the end, everything is H2H (Human to Human), because everything is about people and the value that you are able to offer them through their experience with you. The legal figure with which these people establish their relationships does not change the essence of the relationships between those people, nor their purpose or plan.

The name of her position in the organization. The Intrapreneur is not moved by titles because she has his own title, which is aligned with her purpose, her values, her passions and her talents. The reason why she participates in a project or collaborates with a company is not her job title, but the result of value resulting from that collaboration, having been part of a project capable of transforming reality.

The salary level. For the Intrapreneur, money is never an end but a means. It is never a cause but a consequence. The cause that drives her is her purpose, and money is a consequence of the actions he takes to materialize that purpose in the context of the project and the company. This makes the relationship between the Intrapreneur and the company independent of money, turning it from a purely transactional relationship into a meaningful relationship: fighting for a common purpose. Money is a consequence of the two-way value contributed in that relationship.

The working hours. In the era of globalization and hyper-connectivity, do we all really have to work from Monday to Friday from 9 a.m. to 5 p.m., contributing to large agglomerations, excessive and unnecessary pollution in cities and, among other things, to that daily stress to which we are subjected?

The work place. In the age of total ubiquity, do we all really have to work and every day in a place that has traditionally been purely and exclusively designed for "our professional *self*" to produce? We talk about the fact that we must favor reconciliation with family life, equate the realities of men and women, but, for some reason, we do not address something as simple as trusting and delegating on all workers of a company the responsibility of working every day where they choose.

As we said at the beginning of this book, companies (not only Intrapreneurs) also have a great responsibility when it comes to making this paradigm shift real, promoting day by day this paradigm shift towards a culture of constant transformation and learning, more liquid and flexible, more open and collaborative, more generous, more human-centric, more focused on purpose.

I invite you to reflect on the aspects that matter to you in your relationship with your company and that you align your behavior in congruence with those aspects. Whether it is with your current company or if you are looking for new projects. Ask yourself and ask them:

What is the main reason why I bring in a unique and authentic value as a professional and as a person to this company?

How does this company encourage me professionally and personally?

What joint vision of the world do this company and I have and what are we doing or are we going to do day by day to implement that vision?

What common purpose and values or principles of action drive my company and me?

No ego. No fears. Conscious. Creative. Intrapreneurs are people capable of leading themselves and with the courage to walk out of their comfort zone to help lead more traditional cultures in the transformation of their business and their talent. Congruent with who they are as people and consistent to live it on a daily basis in the environment they choose to help transform. Capable to ask the right questions, and to undertake the search for the answers, expanding their comfort zone.

The world needs more Intrapreneurs, the true ones. People capable of executing their transformation project guided by their purpose and capable of inspiring and creating value for other people by their authenticity and consistency in doing so. In the next chapter, we will see how and why that authenticity is the key of the value capitalization of those Intrapreneurs and of anyone today.

Chapter 23

Authenticity is the currency of the economy of trust.

How to create the foundations to capitalize on the value that you are able to deliver to people.

There is a fantastic chapter in the *Black Mirror* series titled *Nosedive*. In it, Lacie, the young protagonist, lives trying to please everyone, since the evolution of technology allows anyone to score with stars (as we do today, for example, with restaurants), any conversation or interaction with her. Furthermore, society has adopted this scoring mechanism as the official reputation of each individual and it is the indicator used to authorize the purchase of a plane ticket or access to certain environments such as events or parties. Lacie is so obsessed with her score that she has lost the north, she does not know who she is or what she wants in life, she only knows that she wants to score better and for that, she has to please more people.

The *Black Mirror* series is famous for its contrast of what technological evolution allows, will allow or could allow in the future, with the most deeply and humanly negative feelings such as vanity, envy, fear or jealousy, which make those technological advances transform society for the worse. In the case of *Nosedive*, technology is something that is already available and, in some uses, it is globally accepted (the example of the rating of a restaurant that we mentioned before or, taken on a more individual level, the number of stars that you give your Uber driver after any journey). The dilemma arises when Lacie's relationship with all the people in her environment is absolutely conditioned by such technology (applied to the example of the Uber driver, the question would be if he is kind to you because it is his way of being authentic or because he knows that it depends on it whether you give him five stars after the trip and on that, in turn, his salary at the end of the month or, even, keeping his job).

Let us continue with the example of the Uber driver. Imagine now that that person makes a living out of selling fake articles on Wallapop or spreading fake news on their social networks on weekends. Let us not choose such an extreme example. Simply imagine that the algorithms of the social networks he uses determine that that person, based on his behavior, is not a particularly kind person. The question now is: if you had this information at your fingertips, would you take that Uber? We are the example we give.

Companies are also more exposed than ever to this authenticity filter. Just a few decades ago, the two great success factors of a company were its commercial intensity (as it is called, even today, literally its sales force) and its value proposition (product, price, after-sales service, etc.). Today these factors are undoubtedly very relevant. But they are not the only ones. It is pointless for a company to be sold as "the best" o "the cheapest" if that is not what the results of a quick search of that company say, that anyone can do from their smartphone. It is pointless for a brand to advertise itself as customer-centric if it neglects how the production chain of its products affects the environment and therefore society, those customers on whom it is theoretically so focused. It is pointless for a company to say on its website that it believes in diversity and equal opportunities if it actually penalizes the possibilities of women for being mothers, neglects the integration of people with limitations or underemploys people in inhumane conditions.

We live in the digital age. In an increasingly connected world, people have instant access to all kinds of information, and we are increasingly aware of our own values and how the value propositions that any company makes for us are or are not aligned with those values. Authenticity has become the currency of the trust economy. In an increasingly globalized and increasingly digitized world, anyone in the world can do business, carry out a sale and purchase transaction, with anyone in the world thanks to the fact that we are all connected in a huge network. The possibilities are almost endless and we delegate our trust in the network itself, which must establish objective criteria with which to help us decide if that other person is trustworthy or not, based on the data that the network has about that person.

However, people have to make sense of these technological revolutions and the possibilities that are offered to us. We must be critical of our own authenticity as individuals, both with others and with ourselves, in the physical and digital world. In *Nosedive*, Lacie lives an inauthentic life, because she is a slave to the system, to the *Artificial Intelligence* that decides if her reputation is higher or lower based on what other people think of her. The Uber driver in the example lives an inauthentic life, since the only reason he is kind to his customers is because he knows that they are going to feed data to the algorithm that will decide whether to continue doing his job or not. If we gift our personal authenticity to an Instagram profile by collecting a few followers and likes, we live an inauthentic life. If we go to work day after day in a place where for this we have to put on a corporate mask so as not to clash with the average, we live an inauthentic life. But in all cases the authenticity comes to light, illuminating the only reality, over the good or bad reputation that these people have: that they are slaves, because they have given away their freedom to an algorithm, to another intelligence that is *artificial*.

Technology can help us inform the thousands of decisions we make every day, but we should not delegate those decisions to technology. As intelligent beings, we must add our human intelligence to that artificial intelligence that helps us, envelop it with awareness, creativity and ethical principles and values, and we must be the ones who pay attention, are aware, know, learn and make decisions. Starting with those that affect ourselves, no matter how small.

Yuval Noah Harari, historian and renowned author of plays such as *Sapiens, Homo Deus and 21 Lessons for the 21st Century*, wrote in an article entitled *What kids need to learn to succeed in 2050*: "If you don't know what you want in life, it will be too easy for technology to identify your goals and take control of your life." Harari recovers the Socratic principle *know thyself*, the protagonist of so many books, films and hero journeys, and adds a temporary urgency in my critical opinion: today life is digital and digital is life, everything generates data and that data serve as fuel for the learning engines based on Artificial Intelligence that improve the way in which Coca-cola, Nike, McDonalds, your bank, your insurance company, your telephone company or the shopping center you go to in order to at the weekend know you and, therefore, the way in which they can personalize the products, offers and messages with which they are addressed to you so that you "make the decision" to consume them. Algorithms, Artificial Intelligence, know you and know what is most likely to be relevant to you. When Google shows you an ordered result of links for a search, which is different from the order in which it shows those links to another person who has done the same search, Google is deciding what is most relevant to you. Of course, you have the possibility to navigate to the eighth page of results and click on the fifth link, but Google knows that you are not going to do it. One might wonder if we really have the capacity to choose or if Artificial Intelligence is deciding for us what is good and bad.

The same applies to the many decisions that we make daily based on Artificial Intelligence. The route to go to work. The movie that we will see and the food delivery that we will order on a Friday night. The people we decided to meet as potential partner candidates. All are decisions for which technology today already offers us great possibilities. Artificial Intelligence is already present in those apps and digital services such as Google Maps, Netflix, Just Eat or Tinder that people use massively. They are very supportive. But, as human beings, we have to ask ourselves if, in addition to having that technological capacity at our fingertips, we are still capable of getting lost and orienting ourselves, of exploring and discovering new places, of trying a new cinematographic genre or type of cuisine, of meeting new people without an algorithm telling us how compatible they are with us. Because if we have lost those very human habits, the reality is that we have given away our intelligence to Artificial Intelligence, which will be able to make better decisions for us than ourselves.

With the permission of Harari and Socrates, I would like to add the other side of the coin to that principle of life, which is self-knowledge: *be yourself*. As obvious as it may seem, the congruence between who we are and what we do on a daily basis, between our WHAT FOR and our WHATs, is simply something that we can no longer ignore. Knowing yourself implies a *mindful*, serene, lucid, and equanimous awareness of what is good and what is bad for you. But it is only the first step. The one that completes the circle is the action, the experience, the learning and, ultimately, the *being*. Without addiction to the good and without suffering for the bad. With a beginner's mind to continuously learn and with the goal of choosing to do, in an authentic way, what is (relevant) for you. That *mindful* awareness allows you to *be* more *yourself* than the person an algorithm thinks you are.

Evolution must be at the service of human beings, not the other way around. Technology should help people make better decisions, not make them for us. Artificial Intelligence must support Human Intelligence, not replace it.

But people must make the effort not to lose human abilities. The effort of getting lost, exploring and discovering in a new city, despite the fact that Google Maps knows the most efficient route. The effort of trying a new restaurant or a new genre of film, even though Just Eat and Netflix have the best recommendation for those Friday nights of couch and blanket. The effort of meeting people by establishing human relationships, despite the fact that Tinder puts the red carpet in the way of the shortcut.

We must make the effort to *be* human, even though the world is digital. At least, we must not lose the habits that allow us to choose how and when to rely on Artificial Intelligence.

Moreover, we must make the effort to *be* ourselves, and not give our essence, our purpose, our plan, the KPIs of our life, the actions of our day by day and the choices that direct those actions to any other intelligence, although it is also human, holds the title of *boss* and we believe that our salary and therefore our life plan depends on it. If you think about it, giving your intelligence to your *boss* is not far from giving your intelligence to an algorithm: the result is that you stop *being* you to be who another *agent* wants you to be.

In *being*, our authenticity is at stake, as brands, as companies… as humans ultimately. In those action choices that we make day by day, there is the congruence between what we want to be, our WHAT FOR or purpose, and what we are, what we actually do and day by day, our WHATs. And in these action decisions is the basis of the capitalization of any value that these companies or people want to contribute to other people. Because in the digital age, reputation, consistency and authenticity are public assets that every company and every leader must take care of. In other words, in the age of Artificial Intelligence, only authentic business models will survive, with consistent leaders who lead from the inside out: from their authentic example and service to others.

Chapter 24

The leaders of the 21st century.

How to bet on a balanced conscious and creative leadership, generous and sustainable in the long term.

Someone once told me that using, in the 21st century, the expression expresión "of the 21st century" as a synonym for modern or futuristic, sounds like a thing of the 20th century.

The truth is that I agree. Above all, if we stop to think that all those attributes of those that we have called "leaders of the 21st century", existed already in the 20th century, in the 19th and earlier, much earlier. Since the world is world, we have leaders who direct transcendental projects, greater than their own being. Leaders who focus on people before anything else. Leaders who use emotion to bring out emotions. Leaders who, with the utmost responsibility and unbeatable commitment, make the successes of their projects their own successes. Adaptable, empathetic, understanding leaders who put people first, always, in any circumstance. Leaders who are leaders because of their generous doing, which causes the impulse of others and the achievement of collective goals. Leaders who think about the *ourselves* and not so much about the *self*. Leaders who understand that their growth is by contribution of value to a better environment, and not by attribution and extraction of value from an environment in decline. Tenacious leaders in their day-to-day journey, congruent with their values and with unconditional love as a purpose, a purpose as pure as the child who plays for the sake of doing it or the artist who paints for the love of art. I am talking, no doubt, about mothers.

The writer James C. Hunter describes leadership as a paradox: "The art of influencing people to work enthusiastically towards the achievement of objectives for the common good." The paradox is that, for Hunter, the best way to lead is by serving others. The leader is not the first, but the last. Servant leadership. That is exactly what motherhood is.

The moment we live in requires that the authoritarian leadership style based on discipline, efficiency, control and the realization of the *self,* is restricted to the resolution of algorithmic problems, which Artificial Intelligence must progressively take charge of, and embrace , giving way to a leadership style that is more generous, more compassionate, more emotional, more human, more focused on people and on the realization of the *ourselves,* more sustainable, more transcendental, more pure, more maternal. If you allow me the generalization, more feminine and plural.

Every 8th of March, I watch with emotion how the *#InternationalWomensDay* movement grows, claiming those values of diversity and equality, silenced for too long. At the same time, every 9th of March, I contemplate helplessly as the reivindication of those values that reflect our actions on a daily basis, fades.

That the female leader of the 21st century has a voice is not a matter of one day a year or a *hashtag,* but rather that as individuals, as companies and as a society, as leaders, we portray our demand for a more diverse world, more egalitarian and fair, in our day-to-day habits. I intend to introduce a little critical thinking on this very essential topic.

That is why I invite you, employer, to think if, really:

Is proximity to motherhood a deciding factor in your selection processes?

Do you encourage and do not punish reductions in working hours for maternity and paternity, equally?

Do you compensate in the same way the same work to two people with the same profile, but of different gender?

And to you, person/worker, I invite you to think if, really:

Are you defending your values, rights (for example, to your parental leave) and freedom (for example, to work from home and have a more balanced family life), even in the face of your employer, assuming possible consequences that, on the other hand, you consider unfair?

Are you spearheading those values of equality that you defend, also in your day-to-day personal level?

Likewise, I see with enthusiasm the number of social responsibility initiatives that seek sustainability and the common good, of people, communities and the environment, grow. At the same time, I observe how many traditional executive mentalities use these terms as another artificial mask to wrap their short-term lust for individual power, exerting their influence on other people so that they remain blind to the reality that the planet cries out for us.

That is why I invite you, employer, to think if, really:

Are you assuming and acting according to the responsibilities that your company has with the sustainable development goals (SDG) set by the UN with the 2030 horizon?

Do you put the collective good over the individual economic benefit in your day-to-day decisions?

Do you allow and encourage the people who work for you to think long-term, devise a world improved by the positive impact of their company and give them the motivation and resources so that they raise, shape and execute those ideas in the heart of the company?

And to you, person / worker, "consumer", I invite you to think if, really:

Are you being critical, congruent and responsible when defending the values and principles of action of your employer with respect to the sustainable development goals that we should all be concerned about and occupy, regardless of whether your salary may depend on it?

Are you being critical, consistent and responsible when buying and consuming products and services from brands and companies based on how aligned their values and principles of action are with yours?

That the leaders -in feminine plural- of the 21st century have an impact to print a more generous and sustainable leadership, is not only a desirable option, but a need for the survival of the human being and our privileged environment. And just as both women and men can (and should) embody those values of the leaders of the 21st century, I believe that it is the responsibility of both women and men to accelerate this transformation from the reality we live today, and bet that authentic leadership, of the sensitive and generous leaders who give out of love and make others grow and achieve the collective goals, to be a collective human project and with a sustainable positive impact on the world in the long term.

Personally, I have the privilege of living surrounded by leaders of the 21st century, who remind me, as my grandfather did, that being a good leader every day is something greater than myself, and that it is more about giving than receiving. They are the guardians of the trail of my pole star and, without them, it would not have been possible to write this book. Thanks from my heart.

Outro.
A space for reflection.

As after each journey we take some time to rest, accustom our heads to reality, remember, revive and share, I wanted to reserve a good space as the end of this journey to do the same.

If you have lived the journey in the first person, you will have in your backpack, along with your attitude pact, a series of unlearning and learning about yourself and about your reality. Together with them, a series of tools that have helped you with these unlearning and learning, and that at the end of the day are that, tools that, each in its field of action, serve to raise and help solve problems of any field. Use them wisely.

In this space, we are going to go one step further and we are going to observe the journey undertaken, from above. Using abstraction and synthesis to understand why this journey is, in reality, a universal model based on the essence of the human being, and why you, who have traveled this journey, now have the possibility and the responsibility to contribute to its vision of making the world a more human place.

Chapter 25

The leader's journey.

I realized some time ago that the learning process moves human intelligence through a 4-phase cycle, in the face of any challenge that arises. I call this cycle The Cycle of Consciousness, and its phases are:

Unconscious Unconsciousness (UU): I don't know that I don't know.

Conscious Unconsciousness (CU): I know that I don't know.

Conscious Consciousness (CC): I know that I know.

Unconscious Consciousness (UC): I don't know that I know.

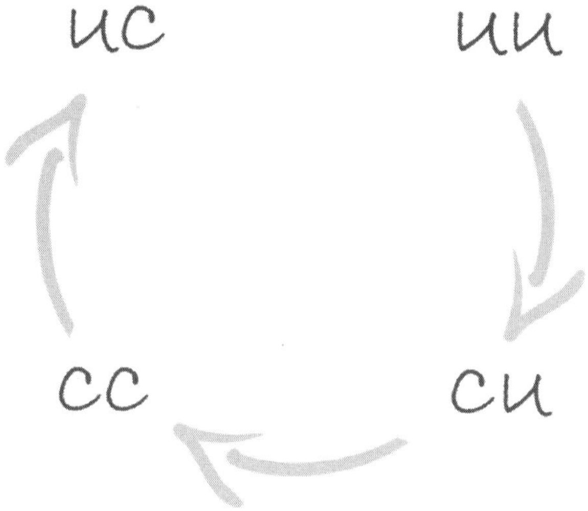

It is a model based on *"the four levels of teaching"* or *"the hierarchy of competence"*, by Martin Broadwell.

Let us see it applied to an example: driving.

When you are a child, you don't know that you don't know how to drive. That is to say: you do not know how to drive and you do not have the need to do so, so you are not aware of the possibility, you don't know that you don't know. In other words: you don't know that you can have the possibility of knowing how to drive. You are in a state of Unconscious Unconsciousness (UU).

At puberty, you become aware that you don't know how to drive. I mean, you know you don't know how to drive. You are unconscious about the action (driving), but aware of the possibility or impossibility of the action (I cannot drive because I am under the legal age to drive and/or because I do not have a driving license). You are in a state of Conscious Unconsciousness (CU).

From the age of 16 or 17 (depending on where you live), let's say, at that same age you get your driving license: you learn how to drive. You know how to drive and you know that you know how to drive. You are aware of the action (driving) and of your ability to do it. You are in a state of Conscious Consciousness (CC).

Finally, after years of driving experience, there comes a point where you know how to drive, in a practically unconscious way. Many expert drivers would even fail the driving test because continued practice generates a habit, a muscle memory, which overwrites many theoretical concepts. This is the state of Unconscious Consciousness (UC). You know how to drive, but you don't know that you know it. Or, put another way, you execute the action (driving) without needing to pay full attention, almost without realizing it, unconsciously.

We could choose other examples of learning to illustrate the cycle of consciousness: learning to speak a language, cooking, living with a person, running a business.

Intelligence goes through these four phases of the cycle of consciousness as learning progresses. And it does it, as we said at the beginning of the journey, seeking its survival and happiness. Seeking to understand reality in order to survive (step from UU to UC) and act on it to transform it and be happy (step from UC to CC). The exploration moves us from UU to CU. Attention and action move us from UC to CC.

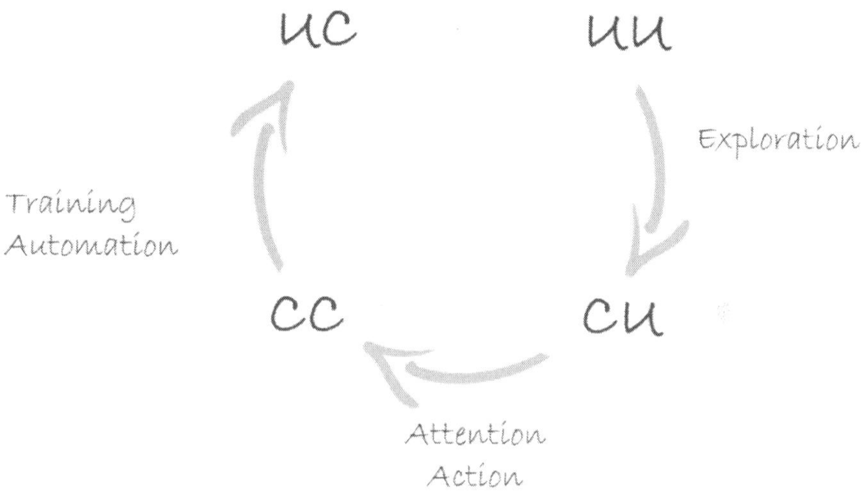

But, in addition, human intelligence does another fascinating operation that I would like to dwell on: the transition from CC to UC. And it does so to optimize its own operating efficiency, as if it was a computer. If my driving state is UC, my mind can perform this task in a *low-power* state and *free up space* for other tasks that are more creative or of greater value to me, such as chatting with the passenger or listening to music, without stopping to carry out the main task with the necessary attention. Simply put, my mind (the so-called working memory) does not need to pay full attention to the task of driving, because it is already used to executing that action, it can do it in a more *intuitive* way, and it puts that spare mental capacity or energy to disposition of another task, or rather, available to me, my own intelligence, to decide whether I want to use that spare mental capacity in another task or not.

Imagine trying to take a final exam or executive presentation without paying full, conscious attention to the task. Impossible. The mind needs all its executive capacity for this task, it cannot be automated. But there are other, less valuable tasks that the human mind can automate. What's more, you need to do it in order to optimize your operating efficiency and keep growing.

Release creativity, does it sound familiar to you? Imagine constantly paying full attention to all the daily actions that we are used to executing from day to day: breathing, walking, driving, typing, eating, etc. We would be highly inefficient, since we would not have the mental capacity for other more creative or value-added tasks on these tasks, which we could call basic.

It might seem that this theory is incoherent with the conscious use of human intelligence, what we call mindful consciousness and on which we have relied as one of the fundamental values of conscious creative human leadership proposed throughout the book. However, this is not the case. The very practice of mindfulness or, rather, as Santiago Segovia suggests, of mindfulness-based meditation, teaches us to be attentive, be aware, *pick up* (know, learn), and later *release.* That is to say, releasing our attention (a scarce mental resource) from those aspects of reality that do not provide enough value or for which we have already acquired enough awareness, to be able to focus it on others. When, through disciplined practice and consistent training, we manage to acquire a level of unconscious consciousness of some aspect of reality, we call this habit, it becomes part of our muscle memory and our "automated" intelligence and we tend to to do it correctly in a more intuitive way. It is true that, in the early stages of mindfulness-based meditation practice, the learner is invited to pay full attention to any everyday object or action, such as a spoon, eating an apple, or brushing your teeth, and this helps him to become aware of attention as a resource of great value. However, in later stages, it is necessary to train in the ability to *release* those aspects of reality that do not require our full attention, either because they do not add value (the example of the spoon), or because we have incorporated it through practice. As a habit to our intelligence, we have *automated* it (the example of driving), and educate ourselves this way in the efficient management of attention as a limited and basic resource of our intellectual development. Let us think about the generation of passive income that we mentioned in chapter 19. This is income that does not need our dedication, our daily work. We can understand active income as the fruit of conscious consciousness (what we devote full attention to, our everyday work) and passive income as the fruit of our unconscious consciousness (what we have automated, which does not require our attention full -our everyday work- because we have been able to generate a habit, in this case, an asset that works for us).

In this way, the cycle of consciousness and, in particular, the ability to automate your intelligence also helps you economically, to generate a business model different from the traditional paid work, to work for you.

After automation, we can also decide to pay *spare* full attention to new aspects of reality that are more interesting, more creative, or more challenging to our intelligence. Imagine that, in your everyday work, you have already developed such a habit that your intelligence has automated many of the mental processes that you need to perform work satisfactorily. One might wonder: Do I need to dedicate 8 hours of my time a day, every day, to this? Or can I do it with the same quality in 6 hours and dedicate my *spare* mental capacity to paying full attention to creating new personal business models? It is possible that the first thing that has come to your mind is the reason why you cannot do that (for example, the limit that the current contractual model imposes with your company). But does it necessarily have to be that way in the future? What is your value in the face of the company, dedicating 8 hours a day, even if some of them are on *automatic pilot,* or the fact of putting all your human intelligence at the service of creating value for that company and its customers? We have already been through that phase of the journey. Let's see it with two more examples.

Let us consider a percussionist in a jazz band. He executes with his arms, with his legs, with his trunk, with his head, with his whole body, dozens of movements per second. If his intelligence had to pay full attention to think about each of those movements before executing them, it would be impossible for him to do it with the speed and expertise that he does. Practice and training have meant that his intelligence has automated many of these tasks and they have become part of it as habits. During a concert, the percussionist looks out for the rhythm, for the turns that the other members of the band decide to make, even of the audience and the context. More creative tasks that are possible thanks to the fact that his conscious intelligence has the available capacity for it. Thanks to automation, the percussionist is more creative in his work. And for this, he previously decided to be more creative, because he had the possibility of being more creative. But it is true that he could have chosen not to take those extra steps, to stay in the acquired mastery and to execute with full attention what he is fully aware of and to which he is already accustomed. Seen from the prism of possibility, it is a shame that he would make the choice not to fully use his talent, but for that he would need to take one more step, which has to be his own decision. Seen from the prism of value, it is obvious that, if his choice is to stay in the acquired mastery (conscious consciousness), his value will decrease very quickly in a context in which his *competitors* choose to continue learning continuously and direct their intelligence towards more creative tasks. I invite you to think about this with your own professional work as an example, instead of the example of the percussionist.

The other example is the well-known confrontation between the then-world chess champion Garri Kasparov and the Deep Blue machine in 1997, which was called "the most spectacular chess duel in history." This was the first time a machine had beaten a world champion (they had met another time in 1996, when Kasparov beat the machine). The game of chess is, ultimately, a huge ramification of possibilities depending on the movements that one and the other player perform in a fixed context (the chessboard, with its 64 squares that alternate black and white), a fixed start (the initial arrangement of the chess pieces on the board) and fixed rules (the allowed movements of each piece, alternate turns, etc.). The machine defeated the human at the moment in which it exceeded the storage capacity of those possible moves and the computing capacity to process them in an acceptable time for the game. However, what not many know about this historic duel is that Deep Blue's power consumption during the game was on the order of thousands of watts, while that of Kasparov's brain was about 20 watts. This is how the neuroscientist Read Montague tells us in his book *Your Brain is (Almost) Perfect*. Similarly, he adds, while the machine required a large number of fans to avoid overheating generated by its computational activity, the human player's brain played the game at normal temperature.

It is obvious that the human being has to execute repetitive tasks. In his daily life, in his daily work. What is not so obvious, judging by how the world has educated and used human intelligence in recent decades, is that we are taking advantage of this human ability to automate tasks (and delegate them, either to unconscious intelligence or to machines) and refocusing that attention and that liberated mental capacity towards more creative tasks.

The fact that Kasparov's brain was playing against the machine at normal temperature tells us that while the machine was at the limit of its capacity, Kasparov had enough mental capacity to have proposed some creative strategy with which to rack his brains and defeat the machine. He obviously did not succeed. However, a very interesting question is what would have happened if the context (board, start, rules) had not been fixed. Would the machine have been able to reprogram itself or readjust to the new context fast enough to continue applying the algorithms of its memory and beat Kasparov? Or would Kasparov have had a competitive advantage to apply those creative strategies, different from the habits and automatisms on the basis of which he was defeated by computing capacity? What if the context changes again? What if it keeps changing continuously? What would happen then?

This is our reality today. The context in which we live is constantly changing and that is why it demands us to constantly relearn. When we acquire consciousness, knowledge and training in a certain discipline, but the context is chaotic and changing, we must take another step. We must not get stuck in the mastery or specialization acquired and train, generate *automated* habits and take advantage of it to release new mental space to continue learning and continue creating. We must not stay in the automated repetition of our acquired comfort zone, but have the necessary attitude to continue wanting to expand it to use our intelligence in a creative way. Constant learning attitude. Attitude of respect and humility in the face of a volatile, uncertain, complex and ambiguous environment. Attitude of curiosity and search for new opportunities. Attitude of doing, learning by doing, transforming attitude, creative attitude. Attitude of starting over and over again. Attitude of leaders without egos and without fears. The attitude that closes the U, the cycle of consciousness, to return to the beginning of the journey. At the same point, but different.

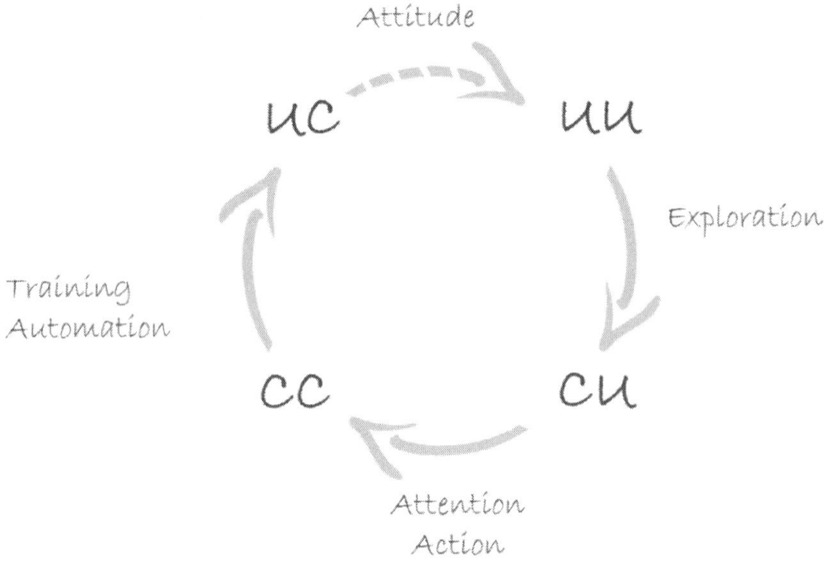

Now let us apply all of this to leadership. According to the MIT (*Massachusetts Institute of Technology*), "during the next decade, Artificial Intelligence will not replace *managers*, but *managers* who use Artificial Intelligence will replace those who don't." For me, this applies both to the knowledge and management of Artificial Intelligence itself as well as to the cycle of consciousness, the use of human intelligence itself, and specifically to automation, to the transition from CC to CU and back again. The training of intelligence so that it is able to automate tasks and release attention and space to dedicate it less to solving algorithmic problems (those that are solved in a certain and systematic way by applying a sequence of steps or algorithm) and more to searching, thinking and solving heuristic problems (those of uncertain context or definition, without a single or complete solution, for which there is no algorithmic way of solution and for which we have to apply creative thinking). Simply put, creative leaders will survive for decades to come.

Creativity again. Creativity as a human differentiator versus algorithmic intelligence: that of machines and (by the way) that of all those who decide to settle for their acquired comfort zone and not use their creative intelligence, stop creating, stop learning.

This differentiator was endorsed by a study by the Boston Consulting Group, which determined that 70% of the jobs that would be created in the future would have to do with creative, non-algorithmic, non-automatable activities, for which the activity of creativity is needed, that of human intelligence. However, it is surprising to observe how even today creativity is a skill sought and desired by educators and parents, but which continues to worry about the uncertainty of the professional future that may be faced by being a lawyer, doctor, engineer or architect. A fact closely related to the fact that in the professional world creativity is considered as a *soft skill* (a soft way of calling complementary skills, desirable, but not critical), versus the *hard skills* that are specialties or degrees, and this ranking continues to determine candidate selections or promotions within companies. Let's call things by their names: specific abilities and human abilities. And let's be clear about the context in which we live: while specific skills will be, little by little and with increasing acceleration, automated and replaced by Artificial Intelligence (as has already happened with previous waves of technological innovation), human skills such as creativity, communication, sensitivity, intuition, empathy, vulnerability, compassion, generosity, appreciation of beauty, emotion, collaboration or critical thinking will continue to be universal and transversal vehicles of connection between people, authentic constituents of Human Intelligence and not replaceable (at least today) by Artificial Intelligence.

Perhaps the hyper-connectivity, the hyper-immediacy, the hyper-consumerism that define the present we live in, are preventing us from seeing it that way. This accelerated context demands quick solutions and that makes us use linear thinking more than ever, in a moment of uncertainty that demands creative thinking more than ever. That is why I understood that in order to release the creativity that is natural in every leader, in every human being, it was necessary to first undertake a journey of consciousness, in the first person, in which we forget about many outdated paradigms that continue to shape our present and conditioning the way we understand the world and ourselves. Only after that journey of consciousness, we can pay full attention to reality to distinguish those aspects of it that really matter in our life, which are essential, and become aware of them to discover our purpose, release all the potential of human abilities that shape our intelligence and put them to work in the direction guided by that purpose to LEAD, with capital letters, the future.

Let us retrace our steps and enjoy the consciousness of The leader's journey:

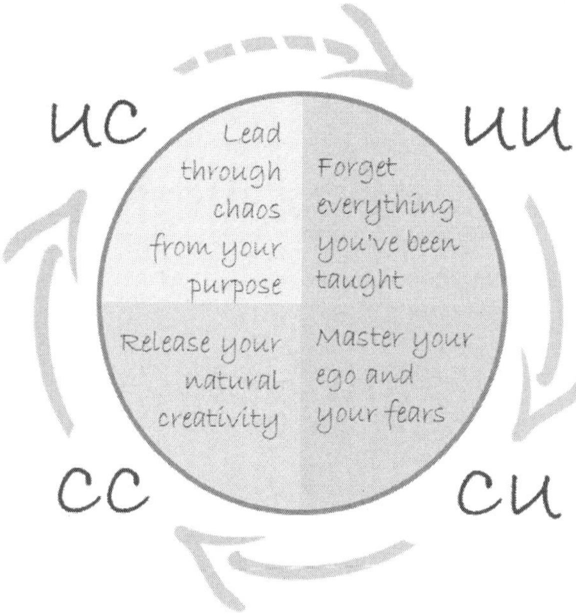

Forget stability and the pursuit of security. Both are paradigms of another century; this century demands leaders who are willing to navigate uncertainty, prioritize the spirit of pursuit of possibilities, and maximize learning.

Forget the secure future. Stop planning what you are going to do or be in 10 years, or 5, or 1, or tomorrow. Context changes too fast to spend your time making rigid plans when variables are simply impossible to predict. Thinking in the key of constant future is the most absurdly simple way to steal your happiness from the present, which is the only thing you have. Focus on the here and now, decide what you want to do, and pay full attention to getting it right. Project the future from the consciousness of the present, with joy and flexibility.

Forget education and serial work. In the era you live in, "serial" is synonymous with automatable and, therefore, you should not consider it a challenge for your intelligence, but something that Artificial Intelligence will solve for you.

Forget choosing between options in a pre-built and limited catalog. Teachers, lawyers, engineers, doctors... these are just labels that you should not indulge in or settle for. The century we live in is looking for new *Leonardos da Vinci of learning*, capable of acquiring specific knowledge of very different subjects quickly, and hybridizing them using creative thinking. There is an excess of impersonal management and there is a lack of leadership by craft, creativity and purpose.

Forget hierarchical structures based on the power of status. Take advantage of the continuous democratization that technology causes, dealing the cards again and again.

Forget everything you've been taught.

Master the ambition of being a title, the name of a position or a salary. In a context in which people will radically change jobs between 10 and 14 times throughout our lives, you must think of yourself as a startup and ask yourself critically why a customer would want to buy your products or services, an investor investing in your growth or society in general benefit from your value proposition, and focus on adding value to all of them; forget the old paradigm of your resume as a collection of titles, positions and salary improvements and build the storydoing of your life based on projects full of courage, passion, mistakes, achievements and learning.

Master the urge to compete with others. In the century that we live in, no one is going to value you for being better than others, but for your capacity for collaboration, alliance, inspiration and natural influence in your relationship with others.

Master sterile envy. Accept the fact that there are things you do not have and want and seek inspiration and learning from those who do.

Master the lack and excess of humility. Know yourself to the point where you do not need to look at yourself continuously and know how to make the most of each context. Be master and apprentice at the same time.

Master the doubts. Find and understand the critical questions that will allow you to make your growth more solid.

Master your ego and your fears.

Release the game. Release the exploration. Release the fun. Release your passions. Release the love of learning. Release the child in you. We live in the era in which professional poses as a badge of seriousness are extinguished and give way to the naturalness with which all people face an uncertain environment, which constantly takes us out of our comfort zone, as when we were children. Your team, your bosses, your customers want to learn from how you learn, not from your pose of success and infinite knowledge. That creativity that emanates from what you are really passionate about is your superpower in the 21st century.

Release meaningful communication. It has only been in the Artificial Intelligence era when humans have realized that we are humans, also in the professional environment. And that humans are moved by emotions. Communicate from emotion and to trigger emotions, from person to person, authentically from who you are and what moves you.

Release your personal finances from needs imposed or invented by a consumption career that forces you to spend more and earn more to maintain a pose of success that has become the boss that no one would want to have. Don't work for him, unlock your economy from that trap. Be aware of the costs you choose and build from there. Work for yourself.

Release your intelligence from the comfort of repetitive tasks, *automatic pilot* and the prison of the number of hours a day that you think do not belong to you because someone else pays you for them. Guide your intelligence towards creative tasks and complex problems. Think, deepen, connect, hybridize and create original solutions. These will be the tax base of your income bills, not the number of hours you have devoted to it. In the age of Artificial Intelligence, there will only be work for creative leaders.

Release your natural creativity.

Lead by giving. Giving means focusing on your customer, on your employee, on your fellow citizen, on the experience that everyone around you has when interacting with you. Think critically about what you offer your customers to get them inspired, just as you demand inspiration from those of whom you are a customer. It is time to open up and give to inspire and encourage others, to be sensitive and generous leaders, understanding that for you to grow, your world has to grow and for that to happen, your place as a leader is at the end of the group pushing and contributing to the collective good, not in front asking for medals.

Lead from your plan. Establish which are the most important KPIs of your life based on the life you want to live, the one guided by your purpose, and simply go for them day by day. It is the age of courage. Changes in context will pivot your plan, but not overwrite your purpose that guides your life.

Lead from your authenticity. Like it or not, in the 21st century your reputation (offline and online) has become part of your history. Reflect on the congruence between who you want to be and who you really are, and think that this gap may be one of the metrics by which this century decides whether or not you are worthy of a certain job. Reflect, deep down, beyond getting that or any job or not: am I living the life I want to live? Am I taking advantage of my creative potential, my authentic essence, no matter how complex and challenging the context to execute is? Am I being the leader in me? Am I adding up to what I feel my mission is in the world?

Lead through chaos from your purpose.

This is *Unleadership*. The journey towards a more human leadership in times of Artificial Intelligence. The cycle of consciousness. The one-way journey to recover the inner and exceptional leadership that the context had made us forget, and the journey back to the everyday world in which to exercise that leadership, with others, contributing to make a more human world. The leader's journey. The awakening of the leaders of the 21st century.

I want to think that this journey and its pilgrims will help many good leaders who are still hidden today.

The good leaders of the present that we live in are self-conscious leaders, who lead in the outer world, chaotic, constantly changing and, unfortunately, many times artificial, because they dominate the inner world, their egos and their fears, and because they know their purpose and their values. They are leaders who communicate from their authentic consciousness to transform the reality around them and create a new better reality for everyone, more in line with what their mind has projected according to their purpose and for the collective good. They lead, they are aware and they create. Creative conscious leadership. Leadership as a conjunction of two aspects: Consciousness or mindfulness and creativity, and in the middle of both our natural capacity and will as human beings to learn and transform.

The best kept secret of the battle between Artificial Intelligence and Human Intelligence is that each person chooses whether there will be a battle or not. We are in the threat phase that any revolution generates, of panic at the possibility that technological evolution will replace our work as humans. But as happened with so many other revolutions in History, the human being embraces change, masters it and uses it to be more. With Artificial Intelligence, it will be no different. The great challenge presented by this revolution is that it threatens our own intelligence, which defines us as human beings. That is why I believe that for Human Intelligence to lead this revolution, it needs a much more profound, personal and liberating journey than on other occasions. A one-way journey to self-awareness, acceptance, and mindfulness. And a journey back to the activation of passions, creativity and continuous learning.

Each person must be free to choose to make their journey or not and to continue doing it day by day.

Chapter 26

The power of not choosing is having choice.

"Choice is an illusion created by those who have power for those who do not have it"

- *Someone with power.*

It may be so. It may be that the system in which we live -education, society, markets- has designed its own survival mechanism, and that the choices that each of us have to make throughout our lives are part of a script prefixed and rigid, whose sole purpose is to perpetuate that system, regardless of what we believe in, what we love, what we are passionate about, or what moves us towards a purpose greater than ourselves.

If we believe that choosing is an illusion, then we are simply slaves of our own being. If we live in such a way that our existence is limited to *executing* in sequence what someone has designed for us, then, we do not actually differ much from Artificial Intelligence by which the system will not take long to replace us.

On the contrary, there are those who choose not to settle. Not settling for an education that is process-centric and designed to produce *students with titles* in series massively, rather than being human-centered and designed for the bigger challenge of teaching us to learn so that we can bring out the best in each of us. Not settling for a society that cares more about our needs as consumers than about our concerns as human beings. Not settling for a business environment that leads more from the ego and individual fear than from the collective purpose.

Not settling is not choosing what is simply part of a script; it is believing in yourself. There begins the authenticity of the leader, with a choice, as small as it may seem. But it is not enough to believe it, it is necessary to act and live in congruence with it, no matter how chaotic the environment continually challenges it.

Everything ends where it started. Exactly the way it started. The context: volatile, uncertain, complex, ambiguous. And you: your conscience, your purpose, your creativity, your action, your authenticity… your leadership. Everything remains the same, but everything is different. Your journey has changed you and you have begun to transform the reality around you, and now you see the same world with different eyes. As in any transformative journey, the important thing is not the destination, but the path. The purpose is not an arrival station, but the pole star that guides us day by day. Because the transcendence of the leader is in the essence of his actions, in what she is. Or, rather, in what she freely chooses to be.

The choices you make day by day from now on are part of your purpose. As small as they are. All your choices build a path that you have designed, because only you know which is the path guided by your purpose, and therefore only you know which choices you should make and which you should not, no matter how much some of those choices are what the environment expects from you.

To a certain extent, I believe that not choosing what is predesigned is the only way to find the most authentic version of oneself. To dominate our ego and our fears to get to know our passions and our talents. To find our purpose. To create and enjoy our own way. To choose to travel it day by day. To be leaders by example, giving the best of ourselves to others. To be happy.

The power of not choosing is having choice. There is something rebellious in that phrase that really captivates me. Perhaps it is because creativity rarely expresses itself in preset environments. Perhaps because Artificial Intelligence does not (yet) know how to rebel. Perhaps because the very name *Unleadership* demanded a humanistic liberation from an alienated industrial existence that should not correspond to the time we live.

I am simply left with the idea that there is no better cause to be rebellious than to live our own life freely.

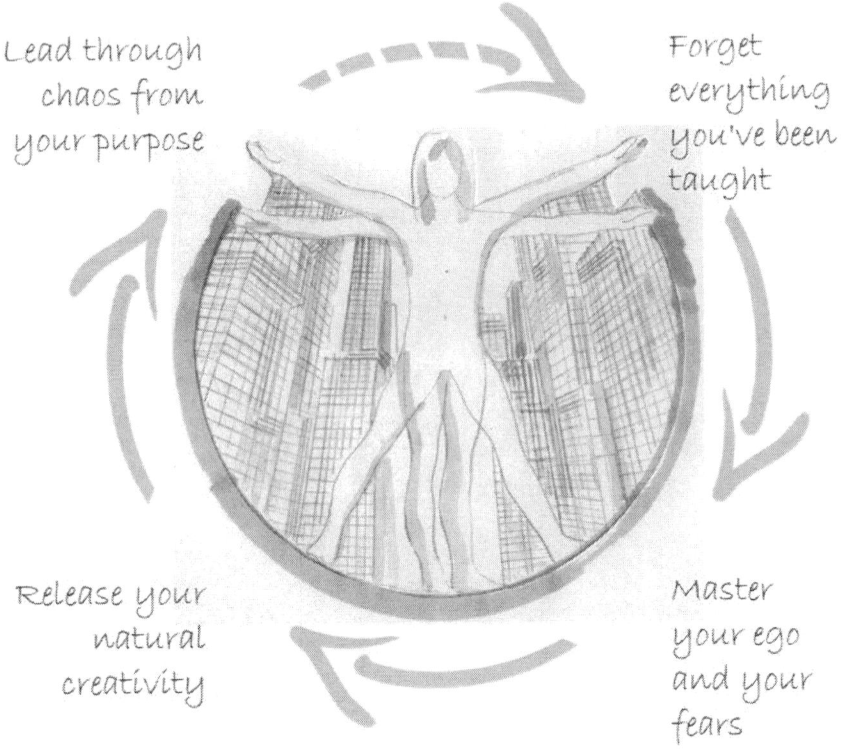
Lead through chaos from your purpose
Forget everything you've been taught
Master your ego and your fears
Release your natural creativity

Balance and understanding lead to freedom from the fear of death. The hero, with his powerful achievement, opts for living in the moment.

Acknowledgements

I have the privilege of living surrounded by so many people to thank for something, that for a long time I thought more about not failing those that I would surely forget in the acknowledgements chapter, than about the enormous gratitude I feel for it being so.

However, generosity is, by definition, shared, there is no leadership without generosity and I firmly believe that the congruence between *being* and *doing* is what gives us authenticity.

Therefore, having mastered my fears, I want to share the name of some people to whom I hope to be showing, day by day, that I am much more grateful to have them around than a few words can express in the acknowledgements chapter of a book.

First of all, I want to thank my travel companion, dance partner, friend, counselor, confidant, support and reference as a person and mother. To the wind under my wings. To my other side of the scale. Thanks Amaya.

To my children, Icíar and Lucas, for sticking smiling suns on my office wall while I was writing this book, reminding me that creative authenticity is a wonderful spark that we adults must fight not to lose and for having been the main protagonists of my journey of deep transformation, the one in which I truly understood that love for others is the best way of being a leader for them.

To my mother, Consuelo, for being everything a leader represents, although she tries not to believe it. For being one of the best guardians of the trail of my pole star and reminding me that unconditional love is the way to happiness, even if I try to forget it.

To my brother, Nacho, for being the strongest person I know and inspiring the world with his intrapersonal intelligence, courage and creativity.

To my uncle, Javi, for acting as a mirror in so many concerns and always being close, "*En copa de balón*"[2], to accompany me.

To Jesús, my grandfather, for each and every word that is written in this book.

To my great family and to my other great family who are my friends, to each and every one of them, for being an authentic and irreplaceable pillar in my life.

To Carmen, for having seen me as a leader in so many moments, but especially at the moment I needed it most, and for her generosity in her efforts to move from *thinking* to *doing* constantly.

Thanks to all the leaders with whom I have had the privilege of collaborating and who have inspired me by their great capacity for human leadership. Carmen, Mari Luz, Agustín, José Ángel, Montse, David F., Tanya, José Manuel, Marco, Manu, Edu, Daniel S., Jaime, Mariano, Caro, Rafa O., Carlos F., Valeria, Nico W., David P., Fernando L., Juliana P., Luz, Pere, Cheng, Gloria.

Thanks to all the people whose stories have inspired me more closely and I have collected in this book: Pepe, Caroline, Curro, Pablo, Lucas. And thanks to all the people whose stories have closely inspired me to reflect on the different issues addressed in this book: Carmen, Luis P., Mosiri, Santi C., Antonella, Raquel R., Héctor, Ana M., Bea C., Daniel M., and all the authors and leaders that I mention in this book, as well as those that I may have forgotten to quote, since their ideas are present in my intelligence, but unconsciously.

---

[2] It is a bar located in Madrid, where my uncle Javi and I usually meet to catch up.

Thanks to all the *leaders of the 20th century* that I have come across in life, because by default I consider them all good people and, from their unconscious mistakes, I managed to better understand some of the main blocks of people and put them at the service of better leadership.

Thanks to all the people whom I failed when I acted as a *leader of the 20th century*, for trusting in my good will despite this, since thanks to seeing me through their gaze I managed to be aware of my mistakes and understand my own blocks to put them at the service of better leadership. I especially want to thank Nuria, Mar, Santi, Víctor, Fer, Alba, Álex, Olga, Cris, Mariele, Patricia and Ángela. And very especially to Inés, Irene, Néstor, Pablo, Diego, Eva, Ana and Álvaro. They know why and I thank them from the bottom of my heart, even though I didn't explain it to them.

Thanks to all who read incomplete versions of this manuscript and gave me their most sincere and generous feedback.

Last but not least, thank you for having read this book and for helping to make the world a place with more conscious, more creative, more human leaders. See you on the way.

Printed in Great Britain
by Amazon

64445293R00108